Beast Mode

How to Be an Alpha Teenager

Shervin A. Azar

The journey is never ending. There's always gonna be growth, improvement, adversity; you just gotta take it all in and do what's right, continue to grow, continue to live in the moment.

- Antonio Brown

© 2019 Shervin A. Azar

All rights reserved.

ISBN: 9781088548561

Shervin appearing on Dragons' Den at the age of 13

Dragons checking out Shervin's book during his pitch

Table of Contents

I. THE HEROES JOURNEY

- Prologue..7
- The journey...23
- The showdown..29
- The unexpected..35
- The panel...39
- Take your chances..41

II. SCHOOLS TURN POTENTIAL BEASTS INTO DEFINITE COWARDS

- What does it mean to be in Beast mode?...................46
- Why am I being harsh on cowards?.........................52
- Where the school comes in!.................................55
- What are the consequences?.................................57
- The Tragedy of the irony!...................................61
- Whyyy???...64
- Freedom or illusion of freedom.............................66
- They don't teach anything...................................69
- Even the smallest details matter............................73
- Hypersensitivity...78
- The danger zone...81

III. THE NEW BEGINNING (Take the red pill)

- Life is depressing and pointless.....................................85
- The dark truth..89
- Why you worrying bucko?......................................100
- No batteries for your Xbox controller, too bad!......................114

IV. TEEN PROBLEMS

- The path to true freedom...119
- The transcendence to immortality...................................123
- Take care of yourself..134
- I'm going to make myself an offer I can't refuse..................137
- Difference between true happiness and being high................142
- Change what you can...146
- Tell the truth even though it might hurt............................155
- Cha Cha Cha Cha Changes!...161
- Peer pressure..164
- Comparison..176
- Time and mind (not an inception reference) 184
- It's the final countdown...190

THE HEROES' JOURNEY

There he was, in a black and silent den, walking down the stairs with his formal shoes which sounded like the heaviest steps he's ever taken in his life, both physically and metaphorically. The Den as silent as it could be, the only thing heard was the sound of the shoes of the young author that's about to face intimidating but silent dragons. As he approaches the six vicious-looking creatures, he thinks of a way to start the pitch and to this day he is still surprised by how he got the opportunity to be there in the first place. Can you guess who this is? You guessed it, it's me!

So, for those of you that have been living under a rock, Dragons' Den is a show where entrepreneurs get a chance to present a product to dragons. These dragons are actually business moguls that will help you expand your product by investing in it and me, going into my fifth year as an immigrant in Canada and literally having the nerve to present my book to these legends themselves, if that doesn't show you that you need to read this book, I don't know what will.

Prologue

See the fact of the matter is, I was basically a loser in life as you'd call it. I was a miserable immigrant; I was so alone that I was always upset but my family always gave me hope and happiness. It was even harder for me because of being an extrovert, but I couldn't talk to anyone because of the language and cultural barrier. We didn't have a lot to work with and we were living in a basement with centipedes in it but I'd act as if nothing was wrong in front of my mom because I cared about her and didn't want her to be worried and upset. However, everybody's life has a turning point except for the green party in Canada. Mine was when I stopped blaming things and tried to be more of an individual, like an ubermensch as Fredrich Nietzsche would call it. How I started, was leaving my weak points, insecurities and worries behind and working on what actually matters in my life which was English back in the times and writing.

When I published my first book, basically nobody knew about it but the deciding factor was how I was going to try to advertise it and how hard I had to work to do it because in life, nobody's going to do your stuff for you because that'd be too easy and life's not easy. In life, nobody's going to chase after your goals and dreams, there is a reason it's called "your" goals and dreams and this is also one of the main reasons some people never succeed and just blame things, instead of running after their dreams and being happy in life. This is what I avoided, if I would've published a book and just had no follow up, I would have been no different than what I was before I wrote my first book. Remember this, your actions define who you are because your actions show what type of personality you have and you can tell a lot just by looking at the person's personality.

That I went on a show where there are six business moguls and tried to present a product/idea or a book and got all six of them, just shows you how hard I worked for that pitch and how much discipline I showed off. Let me tell you that I take my discipline very seriously. Whether if it's motivating people, teaching people about success, writing and you better believe I also take it really tough on my readers, so I can motivate them to be successful in their lives. If you want to continue, just know that only the strong-willed survive after this.

What will this book be about? Beast mode. What is Beast mode? A habit which leads me to everyday success, and I believe that it will also lead you to success in your everyday life.

In this book, I mostly write about the whole idea of beast mode, instead of going into detail about everything because I don't know about you but I personally hate lectures and if you're disappointed that I'm not giving a step by step guide on how to succeed in your life, you're in for a grave surprise because success is mostly discipline and doesn't come in a step by step kit, but more or less I'm giving you the stance I have on life and the perspective I see it in that has gotten me so far in life and I would think that you'd have a strong foundation to start and succeed in your personal lives.

First, let me just start off by saying that if you're not hungry enough, you will never get it. You know what the problem with today's world is? We're all a bunch of lazy humans groaning about success even though we're all just sitting on the couch, binge-watching a movie series.

Some of us are so lazy, even thinking about success makes us feel regretful of our life because we know we can't do it, we're not strong enough to do it, because we're too lazy. To those people, I say put this book away and come back when you have a more serious attitude towards life.

I mean seriously, when you read this section about success and you preconsciously know you're too lazy to do it well, imagine what you'll have accomplished by the time you're in your 50s and 60s. You know why I call these types of people cowards because they're what Friedrich Nietzsche calls the herd.

Most of the population are like the people who follow the crowd, the people who are comfortable, the type of people who don't challenge their style of living or even question morals and ethics in general.

The type of people I want in my book, are the type of people who are extremely hungry for more and people who want to change and welcome change. If you are a coward or part of the herd, I tell you good luck, young sir/mam, because you will never feel satisfaction in your life, you will never know what reaching your limits feels like (it feels really good) and you will always be chasing other people's shadows and trying to fit yourself into society by changing your personality and fitting in and wasting your time by thinking what other people think of you.

In my opinion, that's pathetic and I'll tell you why, if you're changing your personality to fit in with a group of people, then there's nothing to really value in that friendship. Happiness is why we find friends, you can't really be happy when you try to cover up for your socially wrong and flawed personality, you've gotta be who you are and let the people come to you and stop wearing a mask.

I mean seriously, what's the point of being friends with people if you have to change who you are for them to accept you.

Let me tell you this, my last book I wrote when I was eleven and I made it sound like I have a perfect life and everybody likes me but that's not the truth, what is true is that I never went out of my way to change my personality so other people accepted me, I was always weird in a good way.

I am both serious and comedic, at the same time I criticize others and myself a lot because I want to help others and keep on bettering myself in both attitude and life.

I was also pretty naive and inoffensive in my last book but that's going to change because I wrote that book when I was eleven and now, I have a higher IQ and realize that people change not by being sensitive to people but by being serious to people. I also learned that you can only change people who are flexible and want to be changed, other than that you're just trying to move a brick wall.

So if you're one of those people and cowards that gets offended with simple facts and starts to cry when they see a double rainbow because they think it's beautiful, then I don't want you here and I'm serious because in this book we're going to talk about historic facts, philosophy and tips from successful people and their relations to everyday life and we're going to be brutally honest about it. Yes, honesty is brutal but it's the only way to salvation.

You know what else, cowards are losers, they will never get anything out of life than what is given to them, instead of reaching out and trying to get more as a hungry person would.

A hungry person or beast will always be hungry, always want more out of life. Like an eagle preying on a rabbit, they'll be freaking unstoppable, always reaching new levels of success each time. Whether in athletics, knowledge or wealth. As you see, stopping isn't an option for a beast, they will want more out of life, enough isn't enough. When they fail, they will take it as an experience and get back up on their feet, they accept whatever life throws at them, they always try new things and new ways to break the obstacles in front of them, they don't blame others for their own misfortune and accept the fact that it's their own fault like a mature person would.

They always enjoy the sense of adventure and they never think about what others think of them. When things go bad, they adapt to the spot instead of panicking like normal people. All of these are the attributes of beast mode.

A coward or a member of the herd will always be happy with the way things are, won't save money, he or she will always spend until the last dime because they are peer pressured into it or they just don't think about their future and just want to spend money. These people will easily change themselves to suit others and become fake people (I don't like fake people). They will grow up living rent to rent, not having any creativity or skills and being comfortable and fine. They're never winners, they always lose.

If you are one of these cowards that refuses the challenge of adventure in life then don't be overly sensitive and think I'm harsh to you, I hold no grudges against you, it's just I feel sorry for you because if you keep on going like this you will never feel like what it feels like to surpass your limitations and live in the moment or to be a winner. If you truly want to be a beast and not a coward, you must first change your attitude towards life and second, listen to and read everything I'm going to say and write in this book.

If you picked out this book because you at least care a little for your future, good for you, I respect you. On the other hand, if your parents are forcing you to read this because they want to save your future and want you to read this book because they think you're on the wrong path in life and also because they know how hard the real world is, so you can have an easy life when you become an adult and you're still not interested in this book because it's too honest, then don't read it. Go give them back this book and don't say, "I didn't like it", say, "I wasn't strong enough," say, "I'm not ready enough to be a beast", say, "I want to live risk-free like a coward".

If you're upset and insulted by my calling you a coward and loser, come on and rise up!!! Prove me wrong, prove everybody who ever doubted you wrong, change your attitude towards life, read this book and be a beast and prove to anybody who ever disrespected or doubted you that they're in no position to make judgments about your life because a higher level of success always makes you indirectly demand for respect.

Get in that level of Beast mode where nothing can stop you and wake up every day ready for the grind to success, because you will have lots of goals instead of being clueless and being a crash test dummy.

Instead of letting life boss you around, you should boss life around. Make others respect you, not by force but by sheer dignity and discipline.

Get to the level where what others think about you is not important because you know what you see is not what they see, you will know that your goals require so much brainpower, discipline, and integrity that even trying to spend brainpower on what other people think of you is something cheap and unnecessary.

When you turn on your beast mode, you will become so empowering, inspirational and motivational that you will not follow other people but you will create your own path for others to walk upon.

Life will be nothing but a video game set on easy mode for you because you will easily pass through every single challenge life throws at you, whether physical, emotional or mental, you will jump over all the hurdles that life or your adventure has in surprise for you.

In life, those are rewarded that act upon their actions, but can you guess what bystanders get for not acting upon their goals and their dreams? You guessed it, an equivalent of a participation trophy which is a big L on their forehead which represents a nobody! In life, nobody talks about nobodies, in life, nobody talks about losers, in life, people talk about somebodies that actually achieved something and acted on their goals and dreams and made them a reality. In life, people realize and point out people with integrity and hold them as their role models. I guess the same goes for me.

I am a real devil's advocate person and I like looking at stuff from all points of view. The reason that I'm like this is that for a 14-year-old, I've basically had so many experiences, both positive and negative that I've started looking at life in a helicopter's view and have realized that life is a journey and have decided to create an early career for myself. I want to have a head start by using my experiences and since I'm an only child I have had and still have a lot of time to just think in general and move my attention towards things that matter in my life but you see I'm not the type of person to weep with tears of sorrow over my misfortunes, I just forget the past and move forward with all of my remaining strength.

I mean I could talk all day about how we wanted to immigrate to Sweden as a refugee but the immigration lawyer stole our money and we had to go to a much smaller house for one year and how I had to live in a basement that was filled with bugs and centipedes in our first year of Canada. I also don't need to talk about how I moved three provinces in three years changing three schools and how I never had friends because of not knowing English and if I were to put myself in little Shervin's shoes, he wouldn't have been comfortable at the time either, but you know what, I don't really care!

Things got tough, but the difference between the good and the great person is the person who either makes it or breaks it, the legend who gets back up and says after all I've gone through, I can't give up or the coward that stays down after the fall, that's the difference between the coward and the beast. For me, six years have passed and things have never been better. I made it when it mattered and now look at me. You know why making it or breaking it matters? Because this world is about the survival of the fittest, only the strong-willed survive, people who get caught up in their past get ran over by life like a bulldozer. Life is serious and if you try to take it as a joke, you'll probably be the joke.

I'm also not telling you my story so you pity me, because pitying is a waste of time and will get you nowhere in life. I'm just stating that if anyone wants to be negative, they can easily be and blame everything and not continue forward and have a good future.

When I published my first book, basically nobody knew about it but the deciding factor was how I was going to try to advertise it and how hard I had to work to do it because in life, nobody's going to do your stuff for you, that'd be too easy and life's not easy. In life, nobody's going to chase after your goals and dreams, there is a reason it's called "your" goals and dreams, this is also one of the main reasons some people never succeed and just start blaming things, instead of running after their dreams, finding their meanings in this world and have a satisfied life.

I avoided this, being a coward with no discipline. If I would've published a book and just had no follow-ups, I would have been no different than what I was before I wrote my first book. Remember, your actions define who you are because your actions show what type of actions you're willing to take and how dedicated you are to take them.

I take my discipline seriously. Whether if its motivating people, teaching people about success, writing and you better believe I also take it really tough on my readers, so I can motivate them to be successful in their lives. If you want to continue, just know that only the strong-willed survive after this.

What will this book be about? Beast mode. What is beast mode? An ideology which leads me to everyday success and I believe that it will also lead you to success in your everyday life.

In this book, I mostly write about the whole idea of beast mode. One thing you should know is that success isn't a one size fits all approach and if you think that it is you're in for a grave surprise because success is mostly discipline and doesn't come in a step-by-step kit, but more or less I'm giving you the stance I have on life and the perspective I see it in. That has gotten me so far in life and I would think that you'd have a strong foundation to start and succeed in your personal lives.

Now, you might be asking how my journey in Beast mode started, so I'll explain that.

The first thing that happened in my life was that I tried to contact our local newspaper and surprisingly, it worked. I couldn't believe that it had worked, that a young boy like me at 11 could even get an interview with a newspaper, it might seem like really small, but it was a lot for me back then. I felt like I had the whole world at the palm of my hands and that by itself was huge and was basically what changed the outer course of my life and my writing career.

Even when other people doubted me, I never lost my self-confidence, I kept on believing that what I was doing was right because I had trust in myself and had a high ego which is another really important characteristic which I will explain in a second.

I know that you know what self-confidence means, but DO YOU KNOW WHAT IT ACTUALLY MEANS? To have self-confidence, you mostly require assurance, what type of assurance? Assurance as in being sure of the skill you have. So, if I'm an author, I better have the ability to write well and if I can do that, well, that gives me good self-confidence because I have the assurance I can write well. If I can't do that, then I'm not gonna have the assurance that the next time I grab the pencil I'll be able to write as well as I am credited to writing (just kidding, I type).

In life, self-confidence is really important because if you can't have confidence in yourself, how are you expecting others to take you seriously? It's also really important to have self-confidence in jobs that you will have and in the relationships you will make because confidence is also a form of trust. People have to trust you in their jobs, people need to trust you for a successful relationship to take place. So, if you don't have confidence, you will get nowhere in life.

I'm also really sorry to make you cry by telling you that you have to spend effort and time to have high self-confidence. As you might see there's a pattern, in life nothing comes for free and you have to spend effort on anything that you choose to do and be good at in life. When you spend time to develop your self-confidence, you're actually spending time developing your skills and when you become confident enough in those skills, you can say that you have self-confidence in that area and you are eligible to have a high ego in it because with the amount of work you've put into that area, you have the right to puff out your chest and be proud of what you are and alpha everybody out.

Another portion of what self-confidence is believing in what you're doing. You could be really good at what you're doing but still have low self-confidence because you're missing that small portion of belief and let me tell you, even though this is a small portion of self-confidence, it's almost as important as being godly at what you do.

If you're amazing at what you do but you don't believe enough in what you're doing to be assertive or even if confrontation is a challenge in pursuing your dreams, all of the skill you have in that area is basically useless compared to the fact that you can't be assertive about them. Why am I talking about this? Well, because I'm explaining why people doubt and always try to explain to you that you're not worth it and that you'll never achieve your goals.

You know what I've noticed, nobody ever tells you what you can accomplish, they just tell you what you can't accomplish. Nobody ever told me that I'd go on TV twice or that I would be asked by so many places to come and speak, they only told me what I can't do and how I couldn't really get anywhere with this book; even though it was a really good book for my age.

You know why people do that because people are always jealous. It comes back to that jealousy psyche all humans have, their mind can't handle the fact that somebody else is better than them so instead of encouraging themselves to be like that person, they try to discourage the person so they give up and won't get more successful than what they currently are (basically try to bring them down to their level). Now, there is a difference between criticism and jealousy, I take criticism with open arms but even sometimes some criticisms are based on jealousy because you can tell that their criticism isn't really valid.

And it's not like people stopped doubting me and stopped saying I won't achieve my dreams and I won't get more successful as an author than I already am. I still hear it to this day but you know what, the people who have that much brain energy to feel jealousy caused by me instead of spending that energy and becoming successful in whichever area they presume, are also the type of people that eat popcorn with a spoon. But you know what, I'm fine with that, their lack of discipline means one less competitor for me, am I right;).

I will not only let my assertiveness talk but my actions which speak louder than words, I will become a public figure,

New York Times bestseller and world-renowned motivational speaking and I will prove all of them wrong.

But yes, you can easily spot out these types of people who are jealous of you. Even though everybody has some form of accomplishment, people still worry that others will get more successful than them and they have to stop that.

But if these people are jealous I'd like to see them try, I know for certain that if I act like them and have a mindset like them I'll never succeed because I'll be like a hamster on a wheel and be running towards my own demise by focusing on other people more than myself.

The reason I brought this up is there are two types of people in this world, the type that is assertive about their ideas and those who are easily influenced by what others say. This also has a lot of connection with the self-confidence I was talking about.

One of the reasons highly determined and motivated people fail in their area isn't because they were necessarily bad at it, it's because in certain situations they let other people get to them. There are two parts to every ego, self-confidence and belief! Some people do have self-confidence, but they don't have the belief part so they can't really be assertive about what they do. It's really easy to pick on people who don't have the belief part in their ego or don't have self-confidence overall, that's also another reason self-confidence and ego are so important, so you have a type of charisma that nobody dares to challenge.

In any meeting or a public place, I can tell you who has self-confidence and who doesn't because self-confidence relies heavily on the way you talk about something and what your body language tells me. For example, the reason that I'm both a good author and speaker is because of the fact that I spent a lot of time elevating my self-confidence in communication overall, so I'm always ready, prepared and comfortable in any conversation that is brought to me because I have practiced a lot. As you develop in communicational self-confidence, your body language starts slowly forming because with confidence comes a good body language.

For example, you can tell a lot by the way a person is standing or if they are sitting on a chair, how they're breathing, if the speed of the breathing increases, it means its outside of their comfort zone or you've probably done something or touched on a subject that makes them feel uncomfortable. If the breath is heavier it means they are uncomfortable, and you've pushed them too far. If they breathe normally it means they are fine. If they start getting a bit twitchy and you see that they're trying to disengage from the conversation, it's either they feel that you're gonna touch on dangerous topics or just that you're not interesting enough. That was just a few examples of many that I pay attention to in a conversation. I'm always deducing about the person I'm talking to.

Sometimes I might even go really wild and try to see where the other person's pressure point is if it's our first conversation together so I can gather data about the other person.

But yes, so as in me talking about all of this, just remember that you should never listen to what other people do, they're just trying to make you stop feeling good about what you're doing because they know that you're up to something and are up to massive success.

Do you know what the best type of revenge against these types of people is? Massive success is the absolute best way for proving all of those haters wrong, but again, it's not about proving them wrong but proving yourself right, that you can do it and your self-confidence will slowly start to develop and you will slowly build competence.

The Journey

After my interview, which was a huge self-confidence booster, I had to wait because at the time it was Christmas and you can't really make a big move in the break, so I had to chill out a little bit. I still thought about my goals and dreams in life because hey, I'm a dreamer and I kept on planning what I could do next.

So, December break ended and we returned to school. In a move that surprised nobody, I got called to the principal's office, to be honest, I thought I was in trouble, but it turns out that they had read the article and had asked me to make a small presentation for the upcoming new year's assembly. I didn't try to be like an average person and decline the offer because it's "uncomfortable" to do a speech in front of 400 to 800 kids. But the way I saw and still see it, there is no risk. Most people decline on life's greatest offerings because they think there is a risk. Even though the worst thing that could happen (for example in my case) is you forgetting your lines and having to stop the presentation or looking at your cue cards and in this case the worst consequence is public embarrassment which is still retainable but that won't even happen if I build my confidence up with practice. In my opinion, anything other than physical harm is retainable, so it's always worth to take the small risk and to step out of the comfort zone if it means you're achieving something bigger.

And that's the biggest difference maker, people who take those risks are usually the ones who have major breakthroughs in their lives because they're not scared of anything, are full of courage and are willing to make hard decisions for their lives to improve from the state that they're in.

But yeah, I accepted it. I worked on my presentation and was really happy and I'd be lying if I say I wasn't nervous because I was literally presenting one of the biggest projects I had done to a whole bunch of my peers, kind of what you'd call getting exposed.

But yeah, this just pushed my rate of fearlessness further and I also realized a lot of my peers had my back. I got a little bit of competence and realized there was nothing to be worried or scared about in life, they're all just social constructs. Well, unless you're jumping off a 20ft building but that's not the point. I decided this was great but wait what's this.

After my speech, my middle school principal which I still adore to this day came up on the mic and said that they had reserved a place on a panel at the University of Fraser Valley for me to speak about empathy. I was really surprised because they hadn't told me this and had decided to surprise me in front of the whole school which I guess was cool but like now, I had to prepare content for another event, so I was excited.

You see I didn't see this motivational writing and speaking as a job but more of a hobby, a hobby is where you're not forced to do it but you really enjoy doing it. I enjoyed writing about success and doing public speaking about it because I like talking and speaking. I like talking because I'm an extrovert and I like thinking a lot about philosophy, psychology, sociology, etc., you name it so I guess I'm an intellectual, but I have much to learn. Being social was another characteristic that let me learn English really fast.

I always felt alone though, I had no friends because of a huge communicational barrier and couldn't talk to anybody but this also became one of my greatest strengths because I had more time to get comfortable with loneliness and realize what is going on in my life because as an immigrant it's easy to lose track of your life.

Early on since I couldn't communicate with people language-wise in English. I practiced my humor and thought that I could be really comedic and communicate with people better that way and I also started laughing a lot overall and had a lot more positive view towards life. I basically found everything amusing and to this day I still laugh a lot and am really hilarious, if you get the meet me in real life.

So, looking back, what this also taught me was that when a strategy doesn't work, you try other ways to tackle the problem, not the same way. A quote by Tony Robbins perfectly summarizes what I'm trying to explain: "If you do what you've always done, you'll get what you've always gotten"

So, a couple of weeks pass and remember, this is before the university panel then our vice principal calls me to her office again and this time, I'm like is she gonna like get me in trouble so that I can't go to the panel. Like, come up with a stupid reason like you're breathing too much and that creates more condensation than the district limit allows and just suspends me for a week both in school time and out of school time so I have to spend the entire week at the office and can't go to the panel.

Then I sit in the chair with a tight grip on the seat handle as the situation gets more intense.

"Shervin, I need to tell you something". I'm like this is it R.I.P. Shervin this is gonna be the last of me and I'll probably will my Xbox to my dad so he doesn't stay FIFA-less as you'd say. "My superiors have contacted me". Sweat just drips from my forehead, as I know what's gonna happen next was going to the end of me. "My superiors have contacted me, and they want to meet you in person". I looked shocked the droplets of sweat went back into my forehead and everything became confusing to me.

"What," I asked, "we're going to meet with the board of the Abbotsford school district, they have asked for me to bring you to them so they can meet you" she said. Now, everything became clear to as I felt really transcended and cocky, like wow they have demanded to have a meeting with me, woah I'm that important.

But hey, I wasn't nervous anymore so that was something. And the funny part was that when our vice principal was getting into the education system and gradually started climbing her ranks, she had to also do her interview in front of the board, so it was really cool.

At this point, my schedule was honestly busy and for a 12-year-old there was a lot of pressure on me because, you know how a casual 12-year-old life is by just doing his or her homework and maybe having an extra hobby like an instrument or a sport and that's it, they're expected to do good in those classes and that's it, nobody expects more out of them.

for me I had to worry about all of those plus an early career that I had decided to start.

But hey, isn't that what life is about, sacrifices! Only by sacrifices can we become bigger than what we were yesterday. Maybe that requires us to sacrifice our pride to contact a friend we haven't seen in a while so we can maintain a relationship or even sacrifice an hour of video games daily for a greater goal you have or maybe in my case, sacrificing a bit of that safe space to be more successful and popular.

Also, I guess this could be summed up by another quote: "It is a sacrifice I am willing to make"—Farquaad

One of the best examples of this is Dan Lok who is a Chinese multi-millionaire who currently lives in Vancouver and much like me he was an immigrant and now, he's one of the world's richest business consultants.

In one of his books that I was reading, he said that in university he would stay at his own house and read books about the marketing business while people at his university went to parties, drank, whatever they did and basically wasted their time while he kept on increasing his knowledge. In the same book he said that he was basically the invisible kid and he got bullied every day, but one day after he became rich, he was walking through a book store when he saw one of his old university mates. Basically, this was the dude that always partied a lot, and basically wasted his time with friends and girls, while Dan just stayed at home and spent time and effort on himself, learning and researching about marketing. He was working there and he asked Dan how he was doing and how his life was going and since Dan wasn't gonna be a prick, he told him that things were just going good and didn't basically tell him about how he's a multi-millionaire now and just told him that he had a normal life.

But the important part was comparing these two, one of them spent their time wisely and one of them spent their time foolishly. Dan spent time on himself and the popular guy spent his time on other people. It also doesn't mean that Dan was more successful in general just because of his high school period and the other guy turned out on nothing more than a bookstore worker because of his high school period. People really show who they are in high school, so if somebody might waste their time a lot in high school you know that they're not really gonna be that disciplined in their adult life, so this type of behavior will stay with you when you enter adulthood.

But yes, to gain massive success, you must be willing to sacrifice. Back to the story, so by entering in this career I had to give up a little of my comfortable mentality to be more successful and I was preparing for the panel that was happening in a month and the board meeting which was in a couple of days.

The showdown

So, the day came which I had to present my book and my ideas to the board of education of Abbotsford and to be honest I was nervous. Seems like all my plans were forgotten and I was panicking, in moments of panicking you've gotta pull yourself together and get a handle on yourself instead of your emotions getting control over you.

I had lots of moments in my life to get a grip over myself and the situation I was in was no exception. Like for example, I was basically struck with shock when we had planned for years to go to Sweden and then all of our goals and dreams got crushed when the immigration lawyer stole our money.

And the thing that made it even more frightening of a situation was that we had sold everything we had and including our house because in our mind we needed all this money so we could go start a new life in Sweden but it obviously didn't turn out that way and when the immigration lawyer figured out that he couldn't send us, he just stole the money and got off the radar. We had to chase him for a year to even find him. After that, we had to go to court trials and stuff that were totally an absolute headache and were not fair for our part but you know what, life isn't fair you've gotta get used to it. Life is like Donkey Kong, it's gonna keep on throwing barrels at you and you're going to have to jump them!

People think that life is supposed to be enjoyable and it's supposed to be likable. No life is not likable, you'll only enjoy it only when you're successful in the perceived goals in life that are valuable to you and show some sort of challenge, then it is enjoying. Life is supposed to be hard, you're gonna have to wrestle with your problems both mentally and physically and that's also the beauty of life.

There are also mood changes, nothing stays forever. Like yes, we took a big financial fall from that immigration failure, but we didn't just sit there and do nothing. If we would've just sat there and still grieved over our losses and did nothing about it because we thought it would've been impossible to get our money back then guess what, we wouldn't have gotten our money back. But bad times change when you take actions whether if it's towards your goals or in your relationships. That's why in my opinion suicide is pointless, now hear me out, what I just said is controversial, but I actually have pretty deep reasoning behind it.

So, as we all hopefully know by now, humans are impulsive and emotional and this usually gets us in trouble most of the times, but when you rely your life on impulse alone, your life becomes very dangerous. I know I can't imagine what people with suicidal thoughts are going through, but I'm gonna try to put my shoes in their shoes.

Let's just take the worst case scenario, for example, you have a really hard depression, not like small depressions that all teens have but a real hard type of depression, now, I can't imagine what that might feel like but I hope you know whoever is going through should come out about it. Keeping it in yourself is the most dangerous thing you can do in this situation because the human mind is a pretty unreliable source to put your emotions in, you need a third eye, a second opinion as a doctor would say. Ok anyway, you have depression and are feeling really bad and have started to think about suicide because you think that it's the only way to relieve yourself from the sense of uselessness in this meaningless world. Anyway, you think about suicide but I'm here to say why suicide is morally wrong at its core.

Humans wake up with different feelings every day, that's why the human brain can't be trusted, it's always feeling different. So, at a certain period if you're thinking about suicide than that's a bad period in your life. But you've also gotta remember that times change and if you're feeling depressed, you're not gonna probably be depressed in a couple of months or at least if you take the right action to solve it. Same with us, my mom was depressed when that man stole most of our money, literally most of her life was gone but did she just sit there, hell no, you've gotta fight back if you want to feel better.

With the remainder of our money, we rented a little house and bought some small items and started to rebuild our life until we found the lawyer and brought him to court and got our money back. Six months after that initial fall, my mom wasn't depressed, she was happy, we started to rebuild our lives and two years later we applied for Canada. So yes, people change if they want to take actions. So, for that example I used for suicide, there is also a lot of ways to tackle those problems. You have depression, set up a plan and multiple goals on how you're going to solve it. Maybe it's talking to a therapist. Setting up meditation classes and lastly just give yourself time because time solves most things instead of relying on your current extinct to basically suicide, never trust your emotions. Now, that was a pretty adult example of depression and the reason I brought that up wasn't that I think that all problems equal depression, but that even problems such as depression and suicide can be resolved.

I've seen teens that have gotten, in their own words, "depression" because somebody blocked them on Instagram or because they got themselves with their own foot inside some drama like honestly grow up and start using your brain. Stop devaluing mental disorders that actual people have by saying you have them over small problems.

They blocked you, no problem if you cared for that relationship you can put down your pride and go talk to them, if you don't like them then screw them, block them back. Everything in life has solutions even depression and suicidal thoughts, you just need to use your brain and talk it out with people you trust. Even if they blocked you, it's probably because they don't deserve you, don't let everybody into your life and become actually desirable so that people appreciate having a relationship with you. If you spent as much attention on other people as you did on yourself, you'd be the most jacked up, wise and intelligent human being on this planet. So yes, anything is fixable with time, even broken relationships, if you care enough to save them.

So anyway, we got in the car and drove all the way to the board meeting. There, we stood outside of the actual room greeting all the school counselors and just talking with them and I just started small talk with them and honestly, I liked them and they were kind people, I appreciate them for inviting me there.

After a couple of minutes, we entered the room and they sat on their chairs which had a long circular table. To the left side of the room there were a bunch of chairs for visitors to sit on and me, my parents and my old vice principal sat on the chair.

I sat patiently when they were talking and honestly it felt like a corporate meeting. So, we sang the Canadian national anthem and then it was time for them to start their procedures. After like 10 minutes of shaky legs and grinding teeth, I got called up and was asked to start up my presentation.

Basically, the whole point of the presentation was just for them to get them to know me. I finished the presentation and they asked for something that brought a smile to my face which was a photo shoot. So, we did like a group huddle and there I heard the best and most useful compliment I've ever gotten in Canada by one of the school counselors. He said that "we have the future prime minister of Canada right here". It was the best because it just made me really feel good for a few days and made me think about it to this day and honestly that's a lot, considering that I hardly ever remember anything that anyone's ever told me and useful because I didn't know if immigrants could even try to go for the prime minister role but that was just the last confirmation.

Now, I know you're all like ewww politics and honestly, I agree 100%, politics is just gross but honestly, I'm really interested in politics but the thing is most leaders don't even know what they're getting themselves into in the beginnings when they get into politics.

That night I was just overall really hype over the whole thing and we went to a restaurant to celebrate and yes it was great.

But one thing I want to point out here is compliments. Honestly, compliments can make somebody feel good even if they're having a bad day. It can be great morale boosters and confidence boosters and if you're one of those people that needs a reason to do everything that the reasoning you could say behind this is that if you tell it to somebody then somebody will tell you. But overall don't be that person, you don't need someone else's compliment to give a compliment yourself. If everybody complimented each other on a casual basis and was kind to each other this world would be filled with love and peace instead of corruption, hatred, and war.

The unexpected

Around this time, we got a very surprising but interesting email, it was from an executive from girl guides of Canada and it turns out that her daughter went to the same school as I did and was there when I did the assembly and had told her mother. So, in the email, she had invited me to speak at one of their meetings which was another fun event.

I got to see the difference between different stages of life and how each age you see problems differently.

For this presentation in particular, I did what I call a circle in which you make a circular formation by putting people in that formation whether it is on ground or with chairs and then you get a talking piece which can be whatever you want. In this circle the person that has the talking piece has talk and they get to talk for as long as they want, as long as it fits the time table and they get to have that amount of time as a nonjudgmental talk time, talking about whatever they want without anybody judging them.

This is a great time for learning a lesson and a social experiment. What I had planned is to take a huge subject to compare different viewpoints at different ages points which honestly was something really unique on my part.

Anyway, long story short, I went there, did this and it was a pretty good night and I seriously thank girl guides of Canada for having me there. Back to the story, in the circle, I asked a question that was pretty simple but had very different answers to it. I asked about what everybody's different stance was on failure and oh boy, did I get different answers. This showed me a true key point in life I knew and even made myself more determined to solve the problem of which was a motivational crisis. I see that as age increases, our interest in success decreases and at the same time our fear of failure increases dramatically because reality hits us in the face with a frying pan and we have no choice but to let our childhood fantasies go and face a harsh and cruel reality whether if it's in your own personal, relationship or financial life. If we learned how to manage each of these challenges, step by step and gradually the difficulty of these challenges increased than there would be no difficulty. It's exactly like weights, you can't instantly do a 500lb deadlift, you have to start low and increase gradually, but what's happening is all these people are in their late teens are coming to the real world with lots of exaggerated expectations of life and when reality hits them like the 500lb weight and they haven't even picked up a 50lb weight so their life becomes an extreme disaster. And to be honest, my job in life is to make others happy and make them feel good so they can chase their dreams and I'm not asking anybody to be like a billionaire or Olympic athlete, just do something until you're happy with yourself and comfortable and can walk with your shoulders high up proudly.

The type of person that doesn't let others decide how he or she lives, the type of person that has enough knowledge and understanding, in general, to be self-confident so they can have a happy life instead of suffering. Knowing that you're not doing something you've always wanted is mental suffering and mental suffering is the worst suffering. That's why you should not fear failure and take the risk because in order to be a better person and reach your daily goals you have to be willing to take those actions. Even if you fail, it's fine, you have a lot of time, you're still a teen.

As I always do, I was and am already ready for some criticism from adults which I already have gotten, a couple of months after my Dragons' Den airing, I had to do a little article for Dragons' Den. After it got published one of my classmates came up to me and said you should reply to this comment on the Dragon's Den Facebook

So, what am I talking about, well I'm this circle in particular, everybody seemed to have very different views on failure, but they all had one thing in common, they all had at least one positive thing to say about failure. But what was really interesting is that as we age, we become more scared of failures and we take fewer risks in life which diminishes our accomplishments because in life only with risks do you accomplish what you crave. That's why few succeed because risk breeds fear and when you fear something, you won't do it because of the worried sensation that your brain gives you, the brace put the fear away and just do it anyway. However, that this might be a good idea for actual dangerous ideas that you might have, it can heavily backfire in real life because if you're afraid to take risks, then you most likely won't take them and won't be satisfied in life.

However, some adults even contradict what I am saying right now, and I will debunk that right now. After a couple of months, Dragons' Den asked me to write an article about my experience being on the show and after I wrote that, one of my classmates asked me to look at this comment that an adult had left me on that article on Facebook and I was like sure why not. The guy had said that basically everybody says these things when they're young, wait till you're old and one payment away from living in a shelter and you know what, I usually accept criticism but this was crap but you know what, I'm not immature so I don't respond to people on my main account but I would with my spam, just kidding.

But the answer to that is simple and it's to get up off your ass, get a job and save your money and when you're financially stable enough take your next step towards your goal and dream, do it. Being homeless and being in a homeless shelter is a choice, not an absolute outcome. People can always get jobs to stabilize their lives. Anyways, I just wanted to debunk the adult criticism of the idea of risking and failing. Oh, and also if you're smart enough you always have a backup plan other than homeless shelters, feel like I need to clear that up.

The panel

It was finally panel time after a month of practice, I felt like I was ready and I would go and crush my competition, but the friendly competition, that is. Anyway, on that day we also had a group of our students go to the event and be viewers at the event which was really exciting because it was fun knowing I was presenting to them, which was, I guess, cool. So I actually had to wait outside of the main event and practice my lines so I was ready for the questions but I was also nervous since this was my first public event I was speaking at but you know what, speaking was, is and will be my best skill that I've ever developed and back that up with self-confidence and you've got yourself a real powerhouse. So, the speakers got called up and I was actually proud of myself like by a long margin because the youngest person after that was a panelist, was a university student which meant a lot to me because I was the only teen as the panelists.

Ok, so they call out the panelists and then since I practiced a lot, I go there with no nerves and then it was time, I went into my mind palace like Sherlock and sorted out what I would say but yes luckily for me it wasn't a public speech, it was a panel so everybody had to give their opinions, the panel subject was about empathy.

The panel started and then the host started asking questions and everybody took their time to answer the questions and whenever it was my turn, I took my time to answer and made sure that I showed no sign of weakness in how I spoke so I sounded confident. When you sound confident, other people will listen and I had previously thought of pretty intelligent answers, in fact, it was so good that my local newspaper asked me to write a newspaper article which was really interesting and honoring.

Now, remember that this was me when I was a 12-year-old and for an immigrant this is massive amounts of accomplishment and the reason that I'm saying this is because a lot of you are probably wondering that how does a teenager get the motivation to do all of these things and the answer is simple, I just want to prove my worth. In my opinion, proving yourself in life is important because the reason most adults are so unsatisfied in life is because they have not proven themselves to themselves and that's just a really bad feeling because you feel like you have no value or use, you feel as if the universe sees you like the most useless object and pushes you around. Proving my worth goes more than just proving my own expectations, it's to prove my worth to my parents who have made so many sacrifices in immigration alone, it's to prove my worth to my school that's counting on me and the community that's supporting me. When you slowly shift your thinking style like mine, you'll instantly be motivated and be more grateful about the values life has to offer and get up and go after your goals.

This philosophy in life by itself got me this far by the age of 14, I can just imagine how much further it will take me in life as I go.

Take your chances

"You miss 100 percent of the shots you never take"

-Wayne Gretzky

As I have stated like a million times, if you don't take risks as a person, you will never be more than what you are right now and that also goes for risks which have no chance of reducing any resources in your life, then you're literally digging the graves of your goals and dreams for free.

Dreams don't come true by accident. You must work your ass off, so when free risks and opportunities come that don't need you working your ass off, you better take them.

Why am I saying this? Well, after I went to panel, I decided to expand my marketing for my book, so I wrote emails to a bunch of YouTube channels and podcasts so they would bring me on their show and it would basically be content for them and free advertisement for me, so I went to basically in this twilight zone and thought they would all accept me into their show but obviously that's not how life is. So anyways I kept on sending these emails and kept on not getting any emails back and to be honest I got a little disappointed but whenever my mind reminded me of my goal in life, I got the courage and motivation to go again and not give up.

One day a random idea sprung into my mind and I liked it, so I went for it. There was this show on CBC called Our

Vancouver I always watched and it had my favorite reporter in it which is Gloria Makarenko, so I had an idea that would seem impossible for teens at my age because they don't like to aim high; I decided that I would get on TV. Now, this might sound crazy to some of you reading this at home that won't even move even 5 meters to the refrigerator to get the milk, but I had enough courage to write an email to CBC and ask that if I could be on the show. I know that most of you are surprised and trust me I was too, I was questioning my logic, like am I crazy to think that I can even go to TV or what, like for most people going to TV is a huge deal and they wouldn't even try to contact them, but I always see the world from a different perspective and said that I'd give it a try and if it doesn't work, it doesn't matter, I've lost absolutely nothing.

After a couple of days I finally checked my email again, as if it wasn't crazy enough I had a reply, sweat slowly started dripping down and my hands shook and I got myself a glass of water from my room and drank it as if it was the last glass of water I'd ever have and I slowly gulped it down and then I sat on my computer chair. I tried to relax and read it again because I thought it was a reading error. I rolled back and forward on my chair because that's the habit I have when I'm excited/nervous and I reread it. I took my hand off the mouse and put it on my face in a thinking motion and went into deep thought for about five minutes and felt as if time was so slow that it was grating my soul like cheddar cheese every second, I was trying to process what was happening. After the five minutes, I slowly got up from my seat and walked into the living room and asked for my parents' attention regarding something and that they had to come to my room to see it.

They slowly came to my room and my dad read the email and he was truly amazed.

Here's what the email said

"Hi Shervin -- are you able to travel to Vancouver during the school day?

If yes, we'd love to have you here at 12:15 next Wednesday -- you'd be on Our Vancouver (we tape the show on Wednesday) and Gloria wants to interview you for radio as well.

Let me know asap if you can come."

We froze for like 5 minutes until we got the reality of it, *we were extremely* excited but we couldn't shout because it was like 10:30 pm so I literally whispered to my dad, "So what's next?" and after that we had to plan what to do for the show and I started planning content. Now, this is what I was talking about, out of all the times I tried (about 20), finally one of them succeeded and this is the thing you should always do in life, try as many times as you can for the hope of getting one of those opportunities, even better when you have nothing to lose.

Now, imagine if I didn't have the courage to take the risk to write the email to CBC, my life would've been way different, I would have not been able to go to Dragons' Den and I would've never been more than an ordinary teen that doesn't do anything in their lives and the only achievement I'd have is being good at video games. So, what I'm trying to say with each little risk you take and with each time you try and don't succeed, there will be the one time you will succeed. And when you take risks that have no downsides, when you fail or get rejected, then you must indefinitely take them. These risks are what I call shooting in the dark, because when you're shooting in the dark you don't know what you're going to hit but you also know that if you miss there are no downsides and when you do this, you have the chance of that one bullet hit, you will get a boost in success it's like getting hit by a train except success is the train and when it hits you it picks you up and moves you with that speed.

But don't fear if you still don't understand what I'm trying to say, I have one more example of this. I saw an ad in the newspaper one day and it said that Dragons' Den was having an audition tour and it basically going through British Columbia and one city it was going through was Abbotsford, which is the town I'm living in. Then I had the craziest of ideas, what if I actually auditioned my book and actually went on the show and got a deal. Now, at the time it was crazy for me to even consider thinking about this and to be honest I was and still am a dreamer but I'm not delusional like some other people. I work hard for everything that I want to achieve, instead of just thinking about them.

Now, if it was an ordinary person, they would have put the idea on an instant decline because they would have thought it would be impossible for an immigrant that's been in Canada for 5 years to even have a chance to go on the actual show. The panel was something, CBC was another thing but this would be the biggest challenge of my life and I honestly didn't think I'd get on the show but as my philosophy in life goes, I like trying for everything and if I get rejected it doesn't matter I'm shooting in the dark but if I hit the shot than the try I took was worth it.

I did the audition confidently, told them what I had done and they said that if they wanted me to come to Toronto, to be one of the entrepreneurs to present their products to the dragons then they'd call me and sure enough 30 days after, they called my dad and after school, my mom said that we're going to Toronto to shoot an episode and be in Dragon's Den. Each time I doubt or think about giving up, I just think about how every time I was on the brink of doubting myself, I got another opportunity to be more successful by simply accepting that you have to be confident and take the chances even though how impossible and grim they might be. There's always a chance and if you get rejected, keep on taking them until you get that one scenario where you succeed.

SCHOOLS TURN POTENTIAL BEASTS INTO DEFINITE COWARDS

What does it mean to be in Beast mode?

Beast mode cannot be defined in one word but if I were to say it in one word it would be this, Courage. Courage is the thing that takes you from the bottom and raises you to the top. You can't have discipline without courage because you won't take the right chances when it matters. Me taking the audition and writing those emails was a representation of courage. If I didn't have the courage to do those, I would have never gotten the possibility to be popular which would have turned down the motivation for all my hard work, you have to be willing to have both to succeed.

And you know courage and Beast Mode means different things for people. You might be an extreme introvert and be afraid to ask questions and asking a question might be the mark of your bravery and courage and might increase your risk-taking in the micro-processes of you reaching Beast mode.

Courage and Beast Mode are mostly about being brave enough to go out there and giving your life meaning which intern is happiness. Whether that is an ideology, object or person! If it makes you happy and makes you feel like you're worth something, go after it and when you achieve it by going the route that all successful people go, with full consistency without caring about failures and getting back up, that's called

Beast Mode. When that accomplishment means something to you, that means you've done it right and you've obtained true happiness which I will talk about later.

Another question you might ask is how do you get the motivation to have a Beast Mode in every day of your life? And the answer to that is self-motivation, I think of all the people counting on me and how they're counting on me. That makes me motivated to try even harder.

Another thing that helps me draw courage after every failure to succeed is thinking about all the negative with the positive. Thinking about all the people that had a negative impact on my life and doubted me plus thinking to myself, after all I've been through, after all my parents have been through, I will not give up, I will make something of myself so the next day I can walk with my shoulders and chest up high and I can be proud of who I am, what I do and what I present as an individual.

Another question is, am I in Beast Mode? And the answer to that is Beast Mode is different for everybody and for me, yes, I am in Beast Mode. I proved way more than a beast by my own standards, by all the ups and downs I've had as an immigrant and succeeding in the English language this fast and also all the accomplishments I've had from going on CBC all the way to Dragons' Den. As you could see I have proven to be more than trustworthy from what the dragons think of me and the media.

To my own definition I am a beast because, throughout everything that was thrown at me, I proved this world wrong. I proved that I could do it, even though English is the second language I am one of the best speakers at my age and I'm overly eager to show off about it. In life, you must show off about whatever accomplishments and skills you have because if you don't, you will always doubt your skills and buy into criticism from other people and care about what they actually think and they will slow you down.

I'm not even saying be cocky. People are always like no don't show off, be humble, but yes even though some of that might be true, showing off is a normal thing, it also boosts confidence and also why not. If you've got to show it, why not. Showing off is one of the things you should always do when you've accomplished something in the Beast Mode state. With showing off you also get other's respect because let's face it, if you're not going to show off and respect yourself, how are you going to expect others to respect you? Showing off is basically showing the results of your hard work.

You know why else I'm a beast because I'm not a coward/loser. I don't fake my personality so it suits others, I don't care what others think about my goals and work, my biggest accomplishment isn't completing Naruto (don't get me wrong, Naruto is a good show, my friends recommended it but when you only watch something really long with no purpose other than killing time and entertainment purposes, then you should be scared of your current life)

Cowards and losers are the types of people who grow up to be mediocre adults who constantly blame others for their misfortune and never try to change their lives for the better and take responsibility.

Also, according to my boy Dan Lok:

"Being lazy and stupid is worse than being broke. Being lazy and stupid is the lowest you can fall".

Unless your circumstances are or were extremely harsh there should be no reason for you to be poor in a capitalist society unless you're lazy and stupid. Not stupid by nature, but stupid as in you will not even try to open your eyes to the world and try to find new opportunities and just become blind, lazy and just blame other things for your own laziness and lack of discipline. Which also brings me to my next point is that I am in Beast Mode because I'm not lazy and stupid like most cowards who try to brag and show off (even though they have nothing to) and say "I live on the edge and always live my life to the fullest potential" and 10 minutes later they go and sit down on the couch and watch TV. You see talking is the easiest thing to do but taking action and responsibility for those words that come out of your mouth is the hard part.

If you are one of these poor lazy souls and don't want to change, I can't tell you how you'll succeed but I can tell how you will fail You will get nothing new but you will also downgrade. And when you're 18 you will go to university (not even the course you're interested in because you haven't even tried to figure out what you're interested in) and then you will come out of the university and then get a job that's not even related to your degree and then live out the next 10 to 15 years paying university debt off, after that chill until retirement and after that there's death. This is naturally a common stereotype for many people, some things might change like they might not even go to university and go straight to work in franchises and all they will get out of life is a managerial promotion to boost their miserable paychecks by $1000 every month.

However, a beast never gives up even when things look slim and times are tough. A beast has no limits. I went through a lot of tough times from the time we wanted to immigrate to Sweden illegally and then became refugees and then our immigration lawyer stole our money and then we had to go all the way to court sessions to get the money back that we gave him for over one year. All the way to the disgusting centipedes and bugs I had to handle in our basement in Canada and the fact that I was lacking a lot of the language and the cultural barrier to learning the full language and on top of that knowing French now. That's what it means to be a beast, not giving up through the toughest conditions.

I mean it was literary really bad times. We barely made a living. Even as a child I could see the frustration in my parents' eyes because they were making barely anything.

Here's the thing, you might think that I was a child and I didn't understand, but I understood every second of it. On top of that I could find no friends because I didn't know English. It was especially hard because before Canada when I was in Iran, I was a pretty social kid so that was also the cherry on top of the cake for me, a social kid who couldn't communicate. On top of that I moved three times in three years which makes it even harder because you must adapt repeatedly. And finally, when you find that one time where you feel as if your heart is ready to stick with a certain place, school or a group of friends you suddenly have to let it go just for immigration purposes again.

But did I give up? No, like a beast wouldn't, I kept fighting and in five little years I achieved what most adults could only dream of. That's the difference, cowards don't like change, it's a taboo word to them, but a beast is always adaptable like me and will try to use that new environment to his or her advantage. Cowards are losers, they will get nothing out of life and the most outrageous part about is they'll be fine with it. FINE, one word that our modern generation suffers from which I'll get into in a second.

Why am I being harsh on cowards?

"Honesty is a very expensive gift. Don't expect it from cheap people."

Warren Buffett

First, I'm not being harsh on cowards, let's make that clear, I'm being honest and, usually they're both basically the same thing. One fact that gets me worked up about cowards is that they blame a lot of their laziness on others which is predictable but outrageous.

The reason humans put their own lack of discipline and laziness on other people is that they are delusional enough to make themselves the victim of something inside their own head because it's always easier to see yourself as the victim than, to tell the truth, and accept responsibility. Whether if it's someone rich or popular, a friend or a relative, these people will always find something to put it on so at the end, they make themselves feel good and not like it was their own fault because that feels bad and cowards don't want to feel bad because they're narcissistic, sensitive human beings.

They think that if they become the bigger person and accept their failures that it'll be the end of the world! Their tiny human brains can't handle the possibility of failure because we all know how cowards run away from life instead of running towards it like a beast! This is one of the main reasons today's society is such a mess, everybody's so sensitive, nobody challenges themselves to be a more knowledgeable person, nobody has the right to criticize anybody else because the other person will get "hurt" and other nonsense. If you man up about your problems, and actually take responsibility for them and make sure that you don't make the same one later, that's the whole point of failures learning, but if you blame it on others, you're gonna make more mistakes and failures because you haven't learned anything!

Second, these are the type of people who would cry after somebody tells them they don't like them, that's how sensitive cowards are. Beasts are always ready, when things don't go as planned, they sit down, reevaluate the situation and improvise. They won't sit there and cry for three hours straight and dwell in the past but instead take responsibility for what happened, learn so they don't make the same mistake and then strategize for what's ahead in their life!

I honestly can't blame cowards. I have a short story to share about this.

When I came from Iran, I was pretty surprised by how sensitive kids are here and honestly, I blamed the schools. Ok, let me be honest, I love Canadian schools, way better compared to Iran, I don't like the way in general schools teach children and teens. Like they teach nothing about actual life, they just teach lectures that are boring as hell and make you sit in chairs for seven hours a day without letting you communicate with your classmates (even though in the real world your mouth is the thing that makes you money and achieves success because to be successful in life you got to be able to talk properly to others). Then they give you two little breaks between the day and then give you an hour of homework to do every night. Sure, I think this gives you a good work ethic, but it doesn't teach you a damn thing about life and trust me, life is much more about work ethics.

Mark Zuckerberg dropped out of Harvard to pursue Facebook and he didn't get successful by just having a good work ethic, he did it by having a good work ethic and being creative, but schools don't teach that. Pretty much all schools have this standard, but what differed when I came here in western schools was that they made kids overly sensitive and not enough realists! I'm not saying it's the school's fault, oh no, I'm just telling the fact that kids are already sensitive in Western civilizations because everything has instant gratification here, so there are no actual problems because unless you're in mass famine and are going to die out of poorness, (which you can't in Western civilizations because the government literally makes sure even the lower class doesn't suffer that much) in life I would consider any problem fixable. The schools aren't making them emotional, the society is, because life here is comfortable and has instant gratification, but the schools should teach the children how to handle their emotions, because you can make a lot of poor choices when you act upon the judgments of your emotions instead of logic!

What I have realized with schools and people in general everywhere was there was a massive motivation in children and teens, and it decreased as they reached adulthood. I saw a problem with that and sought to fix it and to this day, schools made kids delusional, they showed students side A without showing side B

Where the school comes in!

"I have never let my schooling interfere with my education."

-Mark Twain

In our class, we once had an assignment which was public speaking and we had two months to create a speech on a certain subject. I always found it strange why much of the new generation is so undisciplined yet so arrogant about their lives. According to everybody, they will make the world a great place yet 1% of the population is controlling half of the world's wealth! Don't get me wrong, I love capitalism and the Pareto principle even though there are some flaws but it helps poverty a lot. What I have a problem with is that many people who have the potential to become a millionaire, actor, singer, dancer, and celebrity, but only a small number can reach that and it's the school's fault and parents which also ultimately leads to the school system because they taught the parents . Anyway, I was just thinking on how so many kids, teens, and young adults had this mindset, so I turned my 100% attention towards schools because where do kids, teens and young adults learn everything, school. Sure, you might say that they learned it from their parents too but when the majority has the thinking style that they can change the world with no effort whatsoever, you know its systematic.

You know the problems with the modern western education system is that it makes everybody feel special and tells them that they will all be successful when they grow up but that doesn't happen. They're making kids delusional, that's outrageous. Sure, boosting self-esteem and ego is important and that's literally 50% of the value all successful people follow but where the hell is the other 50%. Why don't you tell kids how hard it is to get so successful in such a tight life with so much competition. Why don't you tell stories of how today's giants got to where they are right now!!! When he was a child Mark Cuban sold garbage bags so he could save up for a pair of shoes, he's the much-acclaimed billionaire and the owner of Dallas Mavericks. JK Rowling, she was rejected by twelve publishers for Harry Potter before she actually landed a deal with someone.

They're ruining society by creating generations after generations of these soft people that can't take the truth and think they can change the world and succeed by just following their passion. NO NO NO, success requires way more than that, you must be disciplined, you must have courage, you require intelligence and you require consistency.

You can't just teach kids/teens like this, oh no, every decision has consequences especially when you're shoving these philosophies down a kid's/teen's throat, Consider the following quote.

What are the consequences?

"For every action, there is an equal force of reaction"

Isaac Newton

When you look at the big picture, these kids are coming out of schools and every one of them has a dream for his or her future. One wants to be an athlete, an actor or maybe one wants to be an entrepreneur and become rich. See all of these kids have these dreams and goals in life and they want to achieve them all. But one of the most important things is that these kids don't know is how actual life works, or do they? As you see, each child will learn what he or she is fed, especially with today's kids where they are too lazy to even read a book and get unbiased information. The schools feed students the types of information about a success that is false. They tell them "you can achieve anything you want in this big bright world as long as you follow your dreams" No!!! That's not true, stop telling lies to children. Dreaming is never enough, teach them that if you value your dream so much, you must take steps and actions for it. (I think this happens less in Canada than in the US.)

So anyway, I don't want to make this a lecture but the consequences are that the children with these beliefs about life grow up and enter this world with the belief that they'll achieve all of their goals and dreams in life only if they follow it, they'll think they become rich, people will acclaim them and yeah, and so on. You know what I call these people, delusional, absolute delusions of success without thinking about all the effort they have to do, and you know what, I don't blame these people. Schools have made them the way they are after all everything has a consequence but this time the school's decisions had the wrong consequences on the current generation and the generations to come.

So, let's continue, they come to the real world with a lot of fake expectations because the schools fed them that. They try to pursue their dreams of getting rich, but they can't because it's hard in this world to achieve success. They question themselves, isn't life supposed to be easy? Aren't you supposed to easily get a 7-figure job? Aren't you supposed to achieve whatever you want in life? Is this just all fake and based on luck? So they just go find a franchise and start working, marry somebody, be unsatisfied with their partner because guess what schools didn't teach how to choose the right partner either and then divorce, but it's a disaster because during the short time marriage period they have had a bunch of kids because they never got taught about responsibilities in life, the kids will be parentless and basically a repeated version of this mediocre life for the kids. The problem with the Middle East and overall Eastern countries is that families are too cultural and take away the kids' freedom, the problem with the West (Canada, USA, etc.) is that since there is so much consumer ship and freedom that you have no struggles in life and this goes for the kids, so kids automatically don't learn responsibility unless they learn it the hard way other than the normal way which is by experiencing trauma and the schools do nothing to teach them about responsibility. They don't teach

Beast Mode

about how important life morals are so then kids turn into these mindless blobs for companies to feed off of which is the ultimate downside to capitalism and consumer heavy societies. In Eastern societies, there are so many problems in life for a child that you learn responsibility by default (there are always exceptions), in the West since there are no serious problems, kids are grown way more fragile. Anyway, the schools teach these students and they become adults and are either A. forced to learn it the hard way and B. just ignore it and suffer whatever problem comes next, they won't have enough responsibility and maturity to endure it.

But the worst part is that these people, the herd, the majority of the population ages feeling sad, regretful and depressed because of the school's mistakes. Schools never helped them find their talents, they thought all the lectures they did will one day help them in real life but it never did. To be honest the own person is kind of at fault here because they never tried to get more information than what was already given to them and try to understand the world better, But you know what numbs the pain of regret and sadness they feel due to lack of moral education from schools, you guessed it, instant gratification. How do you get instant gratification??? It's all around you, internet, TV, Amazon, Netflix, all of these give you instant gratification when you use them, they give you instant pleasure and numb your pain because they're addictive and pretty pleasurable. So that's how people become lazy and like the herd, even if they wanted to follow their goals and dreams, they're too stuck to these instant gratification miracles that would have been impossible for the older generations to imagine.

So, I was fascinated by this whole topic of schools. I decided to do my speech on schools and as I researched more, I realized that I wasn't the only person that thought this way. I realized that the herd or the cowards, it's their fault for the way they are but most of it is because they're the disciple of a wrong corporation. So even though it might be their fault they are lazy right now to show discipline and don't like gaining more knowledge, but the thing is everybody learns from their mentor unless he or she is smart enough to question the mentor's logic in the teaching.

The tragedy of the irony!

"Everybody is a genius, but if you judge a fish, by its ability to climb a tree it will live its whole life believing that it is stupid"

Albert Einstein

First, not every kid should get the same education. Different kids have different circumstances, different dreams, and different needs and then you just put these kids who are all different in this system that only teaches the same damn thing. School teaches the standard things and makes kids/teens believe that their success in real life depends on it and I'm here to tell you it doesn't.

In Finland, students never have homework, there's a teacher for every 12 students, they have only 4 hours of class time every day of which they give about 15 min breaks for every 45 min of work to socialize and communicate and also did I forget to mention they get no tests besides one given when you're a senior in high school! Also, they have much better results from their education than anywhere else in the world!

I'm gonna prove to you how useless normal schools are and I'm gonna prove it to you with two questions!

How do you get successful in school? Take a few seconds and ask yourself this question! I hope you realized that in school you literally get successful by following directions and doing what the teacher tells you.

It's a shock because some facts in life are so simple in life that our brain just simply ignores them, yet they make a huge difference when you see them.

Now, let me ask you another question. How do you get successful in life? Well, this could be a fairly complicated answer because there is a lot of terms to put into action if you want to succeed and get results in life, but let's just give a fairly simple answer. You must have a passion for a goal that will drive your motivation and make you work hard every single day for that passion, so you can achieve that goal and eventually after a lot of tries you will succeed and achieve that goal that you wanted or be lucky and get it on the first try. You will also need a lot of courage to take opportunities as they come! Now, just take 10 minutes and compare school and life in every aspect you can think of!

As you thought, I'm sure you figured out how different these two types of successes are. One is serious for both your mind and soul and the other one is merely mostly for your parent's satisfaction.

At school you just sit in a chair and listen to lectures and do boring projects, all you have to do to succeed is to just listen and follow directions. But in real life, you must be creative, have individuality, strategize and go as planned.

A school teaches nothing about real life to students and just puts them in this boring environment where learning is impossible with no social interaction even though that's what you need to succeed in real life. They kill creativity and destroy individuality but that's what kids need in this modern world if they want to succeed.

I mean, literally how far can you get in today's world if you just follow instructions? If you take away a person's creativity and individuality, they become dull and boring (the common attributes for a coward) And the irony is that they claim to prepare students for the future, even though all the things they teach you just set you up for failure!

Whyyy???

Well, now, you're probably wondering why schools are the way they are, what are they trying to achieve by doing all of this, why are schools set up like this. Well, two simple words, industrial age.

You see the world changed a lot during the industrial revolution and so did schools, since the world was changing quickly and they needed more workers, the school system slowly changed into a worker-friendly place and hostile place for creativity, imagination, and freedom which are all the main characteristics of an actual education. We went from a naturalistic approach to things to a more materialistic approach to things and capitalism.

And honestly, I can't blame them, back then the world really needed workers because the technology and economy were growing every day and the world needed more workers to keep on evolving and boost each country's economy, so the schools started to quickly adapt to suit that lifestyle more!

Thinking about back then, I would've actually encouraged them to do this because we wouldn't be where we are today if it wasn't for the people who worked back then! The industrial revolution completely changed the world and all of our lifestyles. Everything that you can possibly think of, I mean just look around you almost everything is mass made from human-run factories, now, this wouldn't have been possible if it wasn't for the period of industrial revolution.

Beast Mode

Now, I'm not going to teach about history because that's not my job in this book! If you're interested just search it on the internet. My job in this book is to show you how you can get into the Beast Mode that suits you. Beast Mode means both actual success and an emotional balance! Both things schools failed to teach young students which sets them up for a horrible future. However, I'm here to tell you that whatever the schools have done and told you can be undone! And I'm here to give tips on things they don't help you with in life.

I was fine with that type of teaching in the industrial revolution period but in today's world, people with industrial age values don't become successful, I mean honestly, how far can you go by just following instructions? The max you could get out of this world is being a McDonald's manager which is not successful whatsoever. Today's world values imagination, creativity and discipline!

And also, if somehow, you're surprised and still not convinced that schools were changed to make factory workers, I'll show you easily! I'll also show the overall problem with schools!

Freedom or illusion of freedom

In schools, students aren't free. They are what I call modern types of prisoners/slaves of a guilty system that is making society worse and worse every decade.

When kids/teens don't have control over their education, it means they don't feel free and just like a bird in a cage, they will not enjoy it and when you don't enjoy something, you will not do it or in this case, learn it. It's basically enforced education where the system controls the kids, instead of them making a decision. If you're forced to learn something you don't like, you won't, it's as easy as that.

The kids/teens should be able to control their own time as they would in the real world, by taking away the kids'/teens' freedom to decide, you're also taking away one of their most important aspect that is used in real life which is time management. In real life you set up your meetings, your hobbies and chores yourself, nobody's going to chase you around to do work like they would in school.

I'm not even saying let the kids jump around the school like it's a jungle and them acting like monkeys, I'm just saying that students should be able to manage their own time in school on what they learn.

Schools controlling the students' time also sends a bad message to the student, which is that they're not in charge of their own lives (the same message people who work in factories and franchises understand) which carries into the adult life. This also explains why so many adults blame each other for their own misfortunes instead of taking responsibility as a mature person would. Remember, in life, it's always easier to picture yourself as the victim than the actual truth (but in this case they have all the justification because they weren't in charge, they'll just morally blame it easily) that's why there are so many mindless adults in society. Most of these adults never got to feel individuality and responsibility for their lives through no fault of their own.

When you're a kid/teen, you know that the school has your schedule covered so you don't have to worry about that, all you have to worry about are your grades. which is really pathetic, assigning and determining a whole person's intelligence by just a single letter A B C anyway I'll get into that later.

So, while we're in school, all we need are the results, the school will set up and make the structure and what is expected of the students is only results. But when the student comes into the real world, they must set up the structure and also get the results, now, that is hard for the person because schools never taught the students how to put a structure on their time and create a full-on devoted schedule. Now, is this an opportunity to pardon the people who can't manage their time and want to blame it on schools and be cool? OF COURSE not, it would just be a lazy ass excuse. You can't change schools, but you can go explore and learn in the real world. I mean literally, we live in a world where you can learn anything with the touch of your fingers on any device, anywhere and anytime.

It's not like when humans had to go to actual classes to learn stuff, I mean you still do if you want to learn something physically and professionally and want to become a real expert at it like martial arts for example but like 80% of other stuff could be self-taught from the internet, if you have enough discipline to sit your butt on that chair do the thing and have enough self-motivation to do that every day!

They don't teach anything

It would even be acceptable if instead of teaching about success (which they don't even teach about) they would teach about stuff that is actually beneficial. They just give kids lectures and hand them out papers and then follow up with very forgettable tests. WHAT'S THE POINT OF A TEST IF YOU'RE GONNA FORGET IT, HUH? After that, if you get good grades, good for you, you're a good student and quote unquote "smart". First, you're making kids that got a good mark think that they're good at life because they only got a good mark on a paper and their parents are proud of them and in doing that, they become cocky. Second, the people who did bad will think that those marks are actually important and lose all of their self-esteem and confidence when they enter actual life as an adult. So, the main problems are overconfidence and underdeveloped self-esteem for the people that did bad on the tests!

Even if schools cared about students and actually thought things they taught to students would be of use to them in real life, they would follow up with the students that got bad marks, didn't do well on the tests and didn't do their homework instead of making them deal with their parents who have been also raised with the same wrong system and think that marks really matter in life.

What I mean by all of this is even though schools look like they have clear and strict policies and rules, even they don't follow their own guidelines and philosophies of which they pretend to stand for. Like if you value learning so much, why do you leave the kids that don't get as high as marks to rot. I seriously mean it, like I've seen people who don't understand math, they get behind and the schools do nothing about it! They say it is the student's own responsibility to catch up or they must deal with their own parents. This is not learning, this is intimidation.

"Oh kids, if you don't study hard enough in class and don't pay attention in class, well, you're screwed, you're going to have to deal with your parents!"

That is such a stupid way of teaching that it is honestly laughable. If you have an intimidation-based way of teaching, the students won't learn for a long period. No wonder many adults stop learning right after high school or university because schools haven't shown actual learning and the true power of knowledge to them.

I actually have a story on this. I'm decent at math and sort of have a competitive edge in it but I was confused by the move that one teacher made.

So, in Grade 8, our school got a new curriculum and was under new rules and guidelines. It was said to make students more disciplined and give them more freedom, at least that's what I heard. Even though I believed it was not that much of an upgrade, I still liked quite a few aspects of it like the fact that they added a bit more adult-related subjects to the health curriculum to help students with more emotional health!

Back to the story, throughout the year we were handed math assignments and when we did them, our teacher would give us the answers so we can mark it ourselves and she trusted us to tell her the right mark we got, but that's not the worst part (even though this part of the curriculum was really stupid), the move that shocked me was that at the end of the year. We had this huge test that included everything that we had learned in math this year. She told us that if we failed this test, she would put it in our letter grade that she suggests that we take summer school for our math. What are you suggesting?

Now, I have nothing against this teacher, I liked her very much, she was a great teacher no doubt about it but this move of hers looked so fundamentally broken that I had to include it here. As always, it's not the teacher's fault nor the student's fault, it's the system. Not even the flat earth theory has these many errors!

Let me tell you what those words tell me, it tells me that schools don't care for their student's education. Let me tell you what I exactly see.

"Oh, as you know, we're not going to check your homework because we trust that you guys will give the right answer." Six months later: "Oh, I'm sorry, if you don't get a high enough mark in this test you're gonna get screwed, your parents are gonna know and they're gonna get mad and yell at you and sign you up for summer camp."

This just makes students confused, either go with the route of checking the student's homework or just completely go trusting students (which is a horrible idea). What you're essentially telling the students is that you trust in them that they will tell you the right mark they got, but by doing this you're telling them that you still don't trust them and making them deal with their parents. I honestly rather that they check our homework every time instead of doing this because by doing this you're still intimidating the students from the fear of their parents and it's just a bad experience overall for learning and they'll avoid it because when they hear the word learning, they'll get Vietnam flashbacks of schools.

I realize what the school district was trying to do when they did this, they were like "we'll do this to give the student more responsibility so that they will feel more mature and take care more of their work because they feel trusted and this whole system will be based on honesty so that along with responsibility they will develop their sense of honesty."

And I get it, they did this to make sure that the student learned what they actually taught them and they don't really intend to have any type of mental warfare with the students or the feeling of intimidation from their parents, hopefully. But it still screws up the whole feeling of trust and responsibility that schools developed for the students who actually didn't cheat? So, the one thing that seems to make sense about schools, doesn't!

And you've got to realize that I'm not saying to not check it at the end of the year, oh god that's a horrible idea, I'm just saying, don't try to execute an entire idea if you know it has small flaws because even though I don't like schools overall they're still very important and have led the population through the industrial revolution with giving kids the value of factory workers and helping the economy grow. I just don't think that it's right for today's world, the system needs to be improved by a lot and students like you and I can change it.

Even the smallest details matter

Now, I know I'm going to get a lot of criticism and haters for just that bit about schools and you might even say that I'm going too much into detail and am being picky, that it doesn't really affect students and if it does, the students won't even realize! THAT THERE WILL BE NO CONSEQUENCES! Then to those people let me tell you that if it will affect the student's perception of learning or makes them confused, what it will make them, ironically less responsible and lazier.

Now, let me explain how!!! I searched the meaning of responsibility and this is what we got for the exact definition of responsibility, let us explore it, shall we!

I got three definitions for it.

- *The state or fact of having a duty to deal with something or of having control over someone*
- *The state or fact of being accountable or to blame for something*
- *The opportunity or ability to act independently and make decisions without authorization*

Now, let's look at the third point and examine it and relax I know most of you are too lazy to even read so ill highlight important words for you!

- *The opportunity or ability to act independently and make decisions without authorization*

Let's see what our school district got right if they tried to teach kids to be more responsible and don't tell me they weren't they weren't trying to teach discipline and responsibility to students, it's the oldest trick in the book, empower the people who didn't cheat and teach the students who cheated a lesson that whatever you do has consequences.

Okay let's see the first word in the description of responsibility

Ability: Well this is a crappy situation, this test doesn't help any abilities except the fact that your actions have consequences, for the people that cheated which normal schools already teach when you don't do your homework with an intimidation parent-based style.

Act independently: Wow, another important aspect of responsibility which isn't included in the type of teaching that was supposed to teach responsibility and discipline to students. Again, you're making them face their parents, you're not making them realize that they should worry about their own marks. If you truly believe that marks are as important as you make students believe they are. THEY DON'T EVEN FOLLOW THEIR OWN STANDARDS. Students care about their parent's perception of their mark, not the mark they actually get, it has no self-importance to them whatsoever and it's the school's responsibility to change their system and tell parents to encourage their children and make students care more about their marks instead of them overreacting. So, the students feel that their marks actually have a purpose for themselves and not just for showing off in front of their parents. That's how responsibility is developed.

Beast Mode

To be perfectly clear I'm against schools but I'm looking at the school's perspective so that they could actually do what they're supposed to do, what they are meant to do.

The trust problem aside, the parent's intimidation is the huge part of the problem. Now, I said that it makes kids irresponsible and lazy and I can prove that with one word, authority. You see, when you give students authority, they work better, whether it's impressing their parents or having that last strike from their teachers, human beings work better when somebody's bossing them around, that's why success is so hard. When you want success, you need self-motivation, discipline, and creativity, that's why the very few succeed. Nobody bosses you around! Like, imagine if you were given schoolwork under no pressure, no authority, no parents and no nothing, you simply wouldn't do it. Imagine if it was my job to write books, I would certainly do the thing I'm doing faster because my life depended on it, it's money based.

But add parents and teachers and if you wouldn't do it as a teen, your situation would become bad, that's why you do it, you're forced to, you're scared of the authority. So, the students get addicted to this style of learning.

This is the same method used in real life by corporations, otherwise who would want to work, everybody's lazy, it's only because they're forced to so they can buy sardines so they don't starve to death, otherwise I'm pretty sure most people hate working. Honestly go ask anybody who has a boss if they want to punch them in the face!

Now, this is another evidence that schools still create corporate workers, because they are already used to it. People experience authority as a child by schools and adults experience authority by corporate workspaces and authority is usually in corporate workspaces, so schools prepare us for

It's these factors of irresponsibility that makes such lazy adults who have no motivation in life towards their own goals and dreams. The reason students become irresponsible is that after they pass their teenage years and go into adulthood, without authority they can't ever get any work done, because they're not obligated to do it because they have no authority over them. So, they become irresponsible for your own life because you get nothing done and don't feel the need to go after your dreams because nobody's chasing you around like in schools. This is so disastrous for a whole generation I can't even describe it. That's why only a few succeed, they're the type of people that don't need obligation to go follow their dreams, they just do it because they see their vision and end goal and will do whatever they can to get to that end goal! They learn discipline alone!

See, the real reason people succeed isn't that they are a genius, I can show you a lot of genius people with a high IQ working at McDonald's, no. The real reason most people succeed is because of discipline and discipline comes from responsibility. Remember this, anybody can always outmatch a genius with enough discipline. If you're bad at math, spend your free time doing math, bad at science spend your time doing science, bad at anything else spend your time doing that and you get good at it, but the problem is you see the only reason very few succeed is that only the small percentage of the people in the world are not lazy and actually do what they say they're gonna do!

And being lazy breeds blaming. Now that we're talking about it, here's what I think, I actually think that laziness and failure are siblings because they both cause human beings to start blaming anything other than themselves and, as I thought further I actually found a lot of similarities between laziness and failure, because when you try to dream big, your mind tells you that you can't achieve it. Then you become self-aware of the possibility of failure and then you become lazy because you become depressed over the fact that the goal you're thinking about is impossible to achieve. Then when you become lazy, you get hit with the reality that you can't have and never will achieve that goal and as a scientifically proven system of defense our minds ignore to bring the thought that this might be our own fault of not taking actions and replace it with the possible "suspects" that were the cause for our failure. This is another fault of the schools because they don't teach students how to take responsibility for their failures properly. So yes, I think those three words have a lot of connection and that you should never fall in the trap of those three words.

Hypersensitivity

Another dumb problem that schools have is that they're devaluing competition which is a huge problem! Look, I don't want to sound like a hypocrite, I know I said students shouldn't compete for a mark, but this is different, competition for legit stuff in life is understandable and fine. The problem with competition in schools is that first, it's not actual education and second, not everybody starts with the same resource and it's not worth competing for school marks.

Competition is good for humans, it's what drives us to be better. Whether you like it or not, technology is improving by huge companies and businesses (like Samsung and Apple) that are trying to attract more consumers with the competition. However, our new society's problem is that we're hypersensitive to anything that might result in hurting a person's (mental or emotional) state! But to be a better society and better people, we must be able to risk finding out the truth, even if it comes at someone else's expense of getting hurt and if the person is actually smart, they wouldn't be offended by the truth! Learn to accept responsibility for your actions and grow as a person, don't be oversensitive.

So, why did I talk about hypersensitivity if the subject at hand is about school's? It's because this is another one of those important things (competition) that have been taken away from schools because of the hypersensitive society that we live in now. Like they worry that the kids that didn't get as high a mark will feel sad and not as accomplished. The sensation of competition is getting taken away from students from kindergarten to high school.

And you can already see this as the mere stupid existence of a participation trophy! By doing this, you're reducing the value of the person who actually got first place and won and just completely removing the loss factor of the people who came in last place and that's a huge problem! It's good because it teaches and motivates you about how you should change your tactics, habits, and strategies in life! I mean sure, it feels good when you win but you can't always win! Participation trophies make people narcissistic!

Why are you doing this? Are you afraid that the students who didn't get 1st place will be sad and hurt? Well, that's what matures people, defeats! But I'm afraid that society is even too sensitive to get that! In my opinion, the truth is the most important thing in the world, in every aspect of life but guess for some people living the life is easier than trying to find out the truth!

Ok, I'm getting too excited here, what I want to retouch on is the statement I declared at the end of the last chapter! I said that being lazy breeds blaming, because I think lack of true competition and this have a lot to go hand in hand.

The human mind loves the easiest way, it's true! Everybody loves the easy way, but this easily backfires in life when you actually have to spend efforts to accomplish some goals! And the problem is that when students don't learn this in schools, they come into the world with a lot of expectations like "changing the world" but they know nothing about the real world and the same thing happens that I explained in the tragedy of the irony paragraph! They ironically become useless even though schools were supposed to help them get prepared for the real world!

The danger zone

What happens next results from today's society which is going to get worse by time, a society that feels like everything is fine, not daring to challenge modern ideas or modern norms and just going with the flow, just being fine with everything, not challenging their own ideology and beliefs and just not trying to be a better person overall. Basically, the majority of the population is dumb. When someone tries to speak the truth and challenge ideologies as an actual smart person would, they get shut down!

A dream come true for modern companies as they find another sensitive person with no power of self-evaluation or self-thought, feeding into their money cycle. Which is absolutely fine because it's a free market because you have to make people need you to make money, but you don't have to be a part of the herd and just fill yourself with distractions and these companies' schemes.

So basically, the heartbroken person that didn't reach their childhood goals and dreams feeds into this hypersensitive new fine and comfortable society where instant gratification numbs their pain of regret, envy and anger. The difference between the successful person/Beast and the coward is the person who breaks the modern barrier and transcends and finds wealth both material wise and mental wise and stops suffering from irresponsibility and starts doing the right things in their lives and leaves the herd!

The other part of the danger zone is the people that I call weaklings, these are the people that are emotionally weak and unstable adults and don't know how to form meaningful relationships. They make up the majority of the population other than the minority in the population that actually took time to educate themselves on relationships, social and mental problems they get. This is another level that schools fail at, teaching students how to manage relationships and possible emotional problems they might face!

So we end up with more weak adults in society that become a ball and a chain for society to carry, instead of the ones that can improve it, then imagine these people are responsible for the next generation's future because they'll be their parents and what can their children learn from coward parents and schools that absolutely teach you nothing about life. At the same time the level of numbness in society is increasing because the amount of technology and instant gratification is increasing! By each generation, it will keep on getting worse and one day, emotions as we know will just get demolished and everybody will be just blended and emotionless while still blaming their misfortunes on others!

It's amazing to me how easily people get offended when somebody has a different opinion than them and tries to express it! Isn't that how society improves, you might ask? Yes, that's exactly how society improves by asking new questions and improving different aspects of society, but these weak adults haven't learned to respect and judge different opinions because schools didn't teach them that and raised them with the idea of narcissism.

So, at the core of their hearts, these cowards feel like they are the victim of something or more like a system solely designed to make their life miserable and they blame it on that made up system that was made to lie to them and satisfy their unachieved desires, through no fault of their own. This feeling of narcissism that accepting your failures in life will make you not perfect has been socially constructed by schools into the students. It's true, the human natural form likes the ideologically dangerous idea to blame stuff on others due to lack of responsibility, but schools embrace this idea indirectly into students.

It's a fact that humans always like to pretend that they're the victim and the human psyche loves that idea when it knows that it was their own fault, they didn't accomplish something, it gives a certain satisfaction. The best example of this was communism in the Soviet Union and how it worked really well! The system made everybody feel oppressed and victimized and challenged everybody who was rich and successful, so basically, all the people who had actually worked hard on their fortunes and earnings! This also explains why today's society is so sensitive, polarized and super divided!

Everybody has high expectations for themselves, but nobody achieves anything, the schools give high expectations to students but fail to make them realize the reality. Succeeding isn't a common thing, it's actually rare, that's why it holds a special place in our heart when we feel successful in achieving a certain goal we have had for a long time.

Only a few succeed and schools don't make kids realize this and face the reality that's why most fail as a human being after dropping out in high school or university and figure out what actual skills the real world requires.

I will have to be very honest with you, most people reading this book will fail because they have the delusion of having discipline and being in Beast Mode but they aren't. Now, you might ask that isn't there a possibility that everybody reading this who adapts these things into their life will succeed? No, it's way tougher than you think, that's why the 1% controls half the wealth in the world. People with intelligence and discipline make those who don't work for them. That's just the societal structure. So yes, maybe some of you will succeed, but I can assure you that all of you will fail but whoever gets up after that failure and keeps trying is the person who really succeeds. Schools fail to teach this to kids in which case the students grow up to find out that they've been lied to and they can't anything they want but they see that they can't actually do anything so their demand does not meet up with their expectations do they get depression or midlife crisis.

After a lot of thinking you get to the point of not caring about life, does all of this matter? So, what if the schools' systems don't function properly? Aren't we all just gonna die anyway? What's the point of working hard then? And you'd be right, nothing really matters.

THE NEW BEGINNING

"He who has a why to live can almost bear any how."

-Friedrich Nietzsche

Life is depressing and pointless!

Life, is pretty boring, pretty useless when you think about it, but you know what makes it interesting? I'll let you have a guess, not there yet, let me give you a hint, what do video games and life have in similar? They have problems. You see problems are what make life interesting because you must use critical thinking and strategies to tackle those problems. That is the reason life is interesting and amusing.

Now, I said this because many people think that problems are the worst thing in the world and no one should experience them. Honestly yes and no, problems are sometimes really painful and many times difficult to tackle but without them life would be really pale, it would be a big blob of nothingness. Problems give a certain flavor to life, a certain texture, and a sort of added benefit. Now, I will talk about problems and how solving them will be the first step to becoming successful in life. But now, I want to teach you two very core basic things that will help you a lot with problem-solving in your life.

We humans are very passive beings, as I will later on talk about and I say that because we always look at the half empty glass. Most of the times we only see the negative sides of the situations and this is not our problem, this has been indirectly passed through all our generations and ancestors down to us. Which is yes unfortunate but there is a really big point that we're missing and I'll hint it out, what does it mean if an entire generation gains a super strong feeling such as negativity or positivity as their entire personality? It means that their atmosphere, circumstances and interactions have affected their feelings. I think this is for the fact that humans have a genetic social consciousness which is the reason humans are the only living species that have the ability to consciously feel, which means they can express emotions and they can express negativity. All human-related stuff (social interactions, thoughts, the choices you make and what you get from those choices) are all born from two existing human instincts which are positivity and negativity and these two ideologies contribute to everything in our lives, but humans crave negativity more than positivity. It's just a fact because it's just easier to be negative and most humans are lazy which contributes to negativity. Sometimes negativity is okay, maybe you're having a bad day but constant negativity can lead to a lot of longtime problems. Now, it's important that we determine the right terms.

The people that are constantly negative are pessimists and people that are constantly positive are optimists, so pessimists see the negative side to everything and optimists always see the bright side. Everything has its own limits like yeah, optimism is good but too much optimism makes you delusional and makes you forget about reality and also sometimes negativity is good but too much negativity makes you depressed. Now, the following style of thinking that I will explain is called realism, which means you are realistic about everything. You use logic overall to point your positivity so you know when it's the right time to use positivity or negativity.

But as a person who pursues realism in every day of his life, I could tell you that optimism is better than pessimism because in optimism you have a brighter look to life and happiness contributes to optimism but when you're a pessimist you're always sad and feel lonely and the thing is whichever one of these you adapt to your life and brain will be really hard to get rid of so you better start soon.

Being optimistic allows you to find opportunities in your life and to solve your problems, but having a pessimistic approach to things will make you not even try because you constantly worry about what could go wrong and the possibility of the 1% of the failure instead of the 99% of success. It doesn't let you take risks really essential to your life, you will do everything the same way and after a while life will get boring and depressing because you will get bored of being cliché and fear trying anything new. Maybe try out for that sports team you always wanted, raise your hand in class and not consider that the pessimistic side of you might say that you shouldn't do that because the other kids will think you don't get it and that you're stupid because of asking a question and after that you're going to fall off the popular kids chart and where Jacob will be 100% on the list of cool people, I'll go below 0 ahhh!!! Look, I'm not shaming you or the people with this type of thinking and I know you will probably dm me on Instagram and tell me and I quote "it's easier said than done Shervin." I know, ok, I'm in high school so this is pretty common from the pessimistic side of me so believe it or not I sometimes do follow the pessimistic side of myself but not that much.

Just enjoy life while you're young, don't care about what everybody thinks about you unless it actually matters. Use your self-judgment to assess the situation. So yeah, especially in this stage of our lives we should lean more towards the optimistic side but that doesn't mean you can say never be negative, a balance is needed to make these two a healthy combo. But does that really matter in the general picture?

The dark truth

Man - a being in search of meaning.

-Plato

Honestly, you could view reality as a really depressing and boring place because if you see in the core of it all, we just eat, drink and sleep until we die and also get stuck in this endless cycle of working just like a hamster on a wheel. As black mirror Bandersnatch puts it, we're just like Pacman, we're stuck in a maze and there's no way of getting out, there are ghosts chasing after you which are your real-life problems and when you go to the right or the left and you see a way out of the maze you just enter through the other side. So, if you think about it that's how we think when we go into deep thought about the nature of our existence.

In my opinion that is partially true, what am I saying let's be honest with ourselves that is all true but us humans are what give life meaning, we are what gives reality a meaning. Like for example words have absolutely no meanings, you could swear all you want but it's just words, it has absolutely no meaning, it's just a bunch of letters, but it is offensive to some people because humans over time unconsciously decided to give that word a taboo meaning. We over time developed different languages and we decided what meant good and what meant bad, so that's how we based our laws on. We decided that a group of our so-called words would be insulting and it was rude to use that unless we wanted to have direct impacts on the person because taboo words have more impact because they're rare.

As you saw, humans gave it meaning.

But this is just a negative viewpoint, you could also see it as a positive thing from a more positive viewpoint. When humans made communication that's where human emotions started to develop. Things like love and hate don't actually exist, they are things that humans have created based on their other emotions such as anger, sadness, and happiness which were also created by social consciousness and body hormones.

We make relationships because we don't want to have eternal loneliness and ultimately depression by the natural instinct of communication. We've made social media to communicate better. We are the ones who are improving technology.

If you go back, my statement was, yes reality is boring and really pale but humans have tried their best to give this reality a meaning because humans cannot accept this reality as it is and the reason for that is because humans are smarter than other species all the way leading to the 21st century and they know they can always do better and exceed their limits. We knew that what there just wasn't enough for us, so we wanted more and the reason we wanted more is that we had enough self-consciousness and intelligence to recognize that we could progress.

And you could say that we are forced to progress because we have nothing else to do, if we put that away we'll all be depressed and both ways lead to our own self-destruction and that might be a bit true but I think humans are attracted to progress for the exact same reason that you are attracted to it, because reality is meaningless and progress is a form of responsibility that gives it meaning and makes us happy, that's why I personally believe people who don't have responsibility genuinely don't have real happiness.

Progress itself is what keeps the blood in the veins of life flowing, it's the silver lining in the cloud, it's the sunshine after the rain, it's basically pure hope, and just like Stephen hawking's always used to say

"Where there's life, there's hope"

Stephen Hawking

Take this quote but replace hope with progress and it makes absolute sense, progress is just like hope because you know you're always progressing, everything's fine but when you stop progressing that's when you lose hope because you realize you have to face the cruel and dark reality that nothing matters.

It is only when we realized there just wasn't enough for us to do without progress that we had a turnaround, that is why we started to progress more and do better in terms of society and tech wise but that's not all, the next reason is the fact that humans are naturally really lonely species. If we were not to progress than what would we do, basically nothing and humans would start feeling lonely, depressed and bored.

Since the beginning of this species, we would do anything to get distracted from the boring reality of our natural state which was loneliness.

We would do anything to get away from that misery of loneliness. So, we progressed because we were kind of forced to. Like making something called marriage so we don't have to feel lonely by signing a virtual contract that two people sign and are bound to be with each other for the rest of their life. Communication was made because humans had no choice, they were forced to otherwise they had to return to their original form, loneliness. But the most important thing is that humans also made problems too, so life wouldn't get boring and they wouldn't get the hang of the cruel reality and feeling lonely. So, imagine an empty land and then you build a house on it, that is what humans exactly did! They took this land earth and its reality and they built this whole human ideology around it like an insecure bubble that is ready to either enlarge or burst, but that's not all, humans added the competition factor to this whole ideology and added the rich, the poor and other social classes! You create this world where the rich have a normal life and enjoy life and have a lot of workers and the poor try to get rich by working for the people who are rich. It's just like competition and the thing is no one did this on purpose, it was just instinctively, a Pareto principle is what they call it.

So right now, if you want to change in your life you have got to accept the reality we live in a meaningless reality and only by accepting where you're right now in life can you make a change in your habits. Only by realizing that nothing has any moral value whatsoever you figure out that your future is like playdoh and there is really nothing holding you back but yourself. No religion, no others, and no accidents, it's only on you. You accept that responsibility for yourself because you know nobody else will which will ultimately lead you to adopt a form of discipline and responsibility into your life, which also will lead to your happiness. Responsibility is a form of virtue and the reason it makes you happy because it makes you have self-respect, like if I can handle this, then I'm not as useless that I think I am in this meaningless world. You have to accept that the reality is what it is and agree that everything else is just humans trying to forget the true reality that hunts us and make us not feel lonely. You have to accept it right now, because if you don't, you will get bulldozed by it in your 30s, 40s or 50s. You have to accept that even if there's no meaning, in reality, there's nowhere to go but up.

If you adopt the ideology of meaninglessness into your life, it will help you a lot as whenever you're posed with the typical teenage problem you see that it's just really meaningless. You put those away and focus on what life means to you and adopt a form of responsibility and be happy. Teens overall think that they're worthless and weak because nobody can see what their true potential is because the period when you're a teenager is just overall such a mess and there are so many problems you can tackle. It gives you a negative mindset in life and in that mindset you keep on rejecting possible opportunities that might give you meaning/responsibility in your life and make you happier, this book acknowledges this and I am trying to give you pointers and my philosophy on teens nightmares and how to solve them. So you could get that positive Mindshift and finally have a good mentality so you can accept possible opportunities in your life that you always reject because either you think you are not worth it, you don't deserve it, you're not good enough or you're just too lazy to accept opportunities that will make you happier in life..

Now, the reason I started off this book with the whole reality thing is that I believe that if you want to change in your life, whether it's a change in habits or you want a goal you can't achieve, you have got to accept the truth.

I'm trying to make you realize that we can win this game that we socially constructed ourselves. Most things in life are socially constructed by winning I mean, achieving our goals in this life and feeling like a winner. Feeling like you've achieved something, not feeling useless, not feeling regret, feeling like you've done whatever you could've to achieve your goal.

Now, not gonna get too much into philosophy but I'm going to have to show you a little bit of philosophy so the problem can be better addressed.

Arthur Schopenhauer who influenced Friedrich Nietzsche said that the person that has the least suffering in their lives is in the end, the person who has succeeded more according to Schopenhauer, he thought that wealth didn't matter at all, that the person who suffers the least in their own moral structure is the person that will have won the game of life. Self-pity is a big problem amongst teens that make them suffer because they think they're worthless and weak and most teens have this mentality which in turn makes them have low self-confidence. Responsibility in life is the antidote to suffering as I said before because it gives you true happiness. Learn a new language online, learn a new instrument, improve a relationship that you're not so proud of, improve your marks even though they're not that important to me as I said earlier but what they are, all of them is a form of responsibility and when you succeed in a responsibility that means something to you and you truly want makes you tell yourself "wow look at me, as weak and worthless as I am, at least I did this/ that, I learned that new language, I started playing that instrument, I overall improved my mark, I improved some of my relationships". Responsibility turns down the self-pity in you and truly shows what your limits and what you are capable of and that in turn makes you happier.

The funny thing is when you get that responsibility, you are sort of becoming alpha. Other people see the potential in you, they want to work with you, be friends with and because they see themselves lower to you all because you chose to adopt a certain responsibility in your life and they didn't.

It's not that hard, all you have to do is to have a determination and not be lazy. But the real reason I shared this information I got throughout a lot of thinking and research is because when you figure it out, you really start believing you can achieve anything you want because humans created this game, so with enough thinking and help from other people and a little discipline and courage of our own we could easily become good at whatever we pursue (responsibility) at a respectable level.

It's nothing bad, it's just the fact that reality without all the stuff humans added is depressing and really boring. Here's a quote by Friedrich Nietzsche who is one of the best philosophers to ever exist. He challenged things in life such as envy and basically blamed envy for all of the problem's humans faced but he said we should use it to empower our motivations and goals in life and overcome our problems, but I will get to that later in my book. His quote is:

'' To live is to suffer, to survive is to find some meaning in the suffering ''

Friedrich Nietzsche

Now, this basically sums up what I've been trying to say but it's easy to say it now, but back in the time when he was everybody was concerned with politics, war and in general working so they don't get poor and starve to death.

Anyway, enough of Fredrick Nietzsche, now, I'll just focus more on what I was already talking about problems.

So, as I said problems were also created by humans which means if we created them, we could also solve them, so you're in the right place to learn.

Now, when I started to realize the truth of reality I was small but I fully understood it like at 11 and every now and then I take it seriously but it is really important to know the base of reality otherwise you will get blinded and what I mean is that you will forget why we're really on this planet which is to achieve our goals (which is in turn responsibility) while we have the time to feel fulfilled and to have some wild juicy fun along the way and if you don't know or forget you will be blinded by media, politics, and distractions.

By media, in general, I mean news channels and social media which basically control what the people think, especially in western societies.

I don't want you to feel depressed like when I was about figuring out the meaninglessness. I know figuring out that nothing matters is a big stretch, but you can turn this nihilism into a constructive nihilism, if you don't get it, I'll explain. The only reason I told you this is because I want to inform you about life itself and open your eyes and it's because I'm trying to help you because I respect you, I respect anybody that tries to expand their knowledge. The reason is that I care about all teens and try to help them with their daily struggles, and I believe the first step to doing that is to realize the grand design of things and gain more knowledge.

Many people think that we're just teens and we should fool around, play video games and do teen stuff but I beg to differ, yes, we can do those but I believe we should also spend a little time exploring philosophy, nature of life and thinking about our own consciousness basically being in the present because all of those are important. All of those matter in life.

The reason I started this whole thing was that many adults right now aren't satisfied with their situation and the reason for that is because they hadn't started to think about their future when they were your age. I know I said that reality itself is really cruel, sad and boring but with the world and human ideology that humans have made, it will always favor the human which is you. So, if you are actually determined and hungry for the certain goal you have in life you should have no odds against you in this system, especially in western countries, no matter your gender or your race.

If you start to think about your future earlier and what you are in this world and what you want to contribute to it and what you want to be remembered by. We all have a limited time in this world and to be fair it's more pleasing when you know you've accomplished your goal.

So, let me rephrase myself on what I said earlier, problems are fun when you know how to strategize and tackle them and that's the hard part. Problems are painful when you don't know how to solve them, for example: can't get better grades don't know why, don't know how to have a better or even a simple friendship, what should I do if I figure out that one of my friends has a bad habit like smoking or drinking, believe me, all of these problems are really serious problems that a lot of teens struggle a lot with.

I have a lot of problems in life but all problems are resolvable and the thing with problems is that it creates a lot of worrying that will mess with your head and make you not focused on the present. It makes you constantly worry about a future circumstance that doesn't even exist and it gives you anxiety and makes you feel uncomfortable. Now, I'm not against thinking for your own future but what I am against is worrying about a situation in the future that you're not even sure is going to happen and that's the reason why worrying is useless and ineffective whatsoever.

The only way you can tackle your problems is to be positive. Now that I think about it with a sense of positivity, worrying could be really beneficial in certain scenarios if you include the positivity aspect of it.

Like first, worrying tightens your decision making so you think about what you say because you will also be more rational with worrying in your decision making and for the most part, not every single human is rational in decision making. Worrying makes you more aware of your surrounding and decisions including, it's a good thing to keep in the back of your mind.

Second, you pay way more attention to details because you feel like if you don't, you will screw up on something which could be really useful in real life. So, worrying has its pros and optimistic sides but the downsides far outmatch the other side as I will explain in the next section of Beast Mode.

Why you worrying bucko?

"The biggest risk is not to take any risks"

-Mark Zuckerberg

In my opinion, everyone only has one seemingly short unreplaceable life and also my insight on that unreplaceable short life is that you should spend it wisely and live it to the fullest because it's one ticket in and one ticket out. Let me rephrase that, have you ever gone to one of those fancies, over lighted and pleasurable carnivals. If you have, then you know that for each ride, you have to pay with a ticket that you've pre-purchased from the stall. You pay a ticket to get to go in, but you're not allowed to stay on that ride forever because it ends somewhere but it is also a very exciting, amusing and awesome ride and somewhere down the line on the ride it might get obnoxious, surprising or uncomfortable and you might get scared at some points in it.

You surprisingly might feel like you're pressured and you need a shoulder to cry on which is ok, those are normal human emotions, but the point is, when it finishes you no longer have or will ever have the opportunity to get on that ride because you no longer have the privilege of having another ticket because that's just how it works. You only have one ticket and one chance to try this amusing, awesome and long ride (unless you pay again) but when it is over you no longer have a second chance. You could argue if that's fair or not but that's just the way it is, you can't really do anything about it just like how chocolate milk is so smooth, bold and delicious or like how kale is so irresistibly green, crunchy and disgusting. Just like my scenario you can't change these scenarios either, you can't change how delicious and overrated chocolate milk is and how disgusting and unpopular kale is. There are just some things we can't change. My job as a successful author of books for teens, oh boy that was a long name, I'll just call it ASAOBFT. My job as an ASAOBFT is to decrease anxiety, depression, worrying and increasing failures, creativity and risking for my fellow teens. The first three I said are pretty common in teen years, don't know maybe because they are starting to get more mature and the last three, in my opinion, are the most important skills when you're transitioning into adulthood.

A lot of you might be confused by my saying increase failures which I will get into in a minute but before that let me get into the first section I was talking about. There are some things we just can't change but instead, we worry about why we can't change them which in my opinion is natural but also very unnecessary, like why would you worry about that. If you can't change it, you can't change it so don't worry because all worrying does is just screw up your brain, especially at this age worrying is the equivalent of cancer for the brain. In fact, all of the things I said for the first one is equivalent of cancer for the brain but the three things I said to increase, all relate to developing more maturity in you and in others around you. When you start becoming more mentally mature, that's when you actually grow up. Knowledge is not defined by how old you are, if anyone says that then they are no farther away from the truth than an average mind who watches keeping up with the Kardashians because you could be an adult but still not be as smart as a child who has more information about life than you and who can make better decisions.

That's just a really wrong fixation with today's society. So anyway, back to my story on the amusement park. Did you see how many similarities that had with the way real life works, like those huge emotion shifts which were there, those are what defines humans as wholes, it's all right if you feel scared, lost or sad that is fine, those are normal, I feel all of those emotions every day and its fine cause I'm a human and it's also fine if you feel emotions, they describe our personality and are a way to express ourselves, they show us our true colors. they in some sense give us meaning.

I mean could you just take a second to imagine a world where emotions don't exist. Just imagine that and everything emotions helped create like music, colors or movies or even strong relationships. Every single relationship depends on every single emotion that exists. And if you're confused why I said colors without an explanation it's because I did say colors without an explanation so quote Shervin on this Buzzfeed "Deal with it". I know it's a hard quote to understand and its very philosophical and serious but it's my flavor of quotes and you'll get it when you're older.

But no seriously, the reason I said colors is because without emotions you won't comprehend the true feeling of colors like how blue gives you a calm feeling or how green gives you that peaceful feeling and no, calm and peaceful are not the same thing. Or red, it gives you that violent feeling like you're a fighter because of it sort of looks like blood.

So yeah if you look at it everything is directed with our emotions. Emotions are what lead us to a better future. If we learn to control our emotions wisely, we can be in the highest possessions that's what either makes us positive, negative, motivated or bored and that is what I'm trying to get into. I am trying to show you how self-motivation works because if you understand how self-motivation works, you're a beast, you cannot be stopped you will be like a flex tape and Dwayne Johnson hybrid.

But it is possible, and I am sure you will get there if you follow my tips. So, let's go over some of the common human emotions, shall we? Happiness, pretty common everyone needs it, can't live without it. Sadness still pretty common you need it a lot. Now, this one is the important one, fear, pretty normal, right, what if I told you to fear in your personal lives is a huge problem. So, let's take a look back at when I said increase failures, I am pretty sure everybody got confused when I said that and you took a long reflection and thought about what I meant.

Well, what I meant by that is to increase learning because every failure teaches you something and you have to use those teachings to your advantage. In my opinion, what fear does is disable our ability to fail.

Not only that, but what fear also does is that it disables our ability to take risks and grow. It forces us to never succeed to never have the taste of true knowledge or what it feels like to learn and all of these that I'm saying because fear disables the ability to fail and when you don't fail you don't learn anything new and not learning is the equivalent of doing nothing, you get the idea. Not only that but even in our society, failure is not accepted, when someone fails, they believe it's the end of the world, even the idea of accepting failure is not accepted or respected because this is how the world works.

Let me explain it to you by one of the stories of the great Plato himself. If you do not know who Plato is, I just suggest that you rethink your whole life and realize when did celebrities become more famous than one of the most famous, smartest and awesome philosophers in the whole world. Unfortunately for us, the legend Plato himself is dead now, but he will always be remembered of how he tried to open other people's vision about how this world works and how we should think differently about our world. Of course, I know this story won't be as good as my quote that's going to be published in BuzzFeed but it's acceptable (Sarcasm) Plato describes a group of people who have lived chained to the wall of a cave for all of their lives. Just facing at a wall. No modern convenience, YouTube or Netflix so they can binge-watch Riverdale or gray's anatomy on just a wall. And throughout their whole lives, there also was a fire behind them, and they could clearly see shadows of themselves in front of them. They also gave names to these shadows which is pretty sad, but we'll just leave that be, sometimes you are forced to do something because your circumstance force you to and it's not your fault. Like if you were born in a family that is poor, it's not your fault but if you grow up and that hasn't still changed, now, that's your fault but I will touch on that later. So just forget everything and let's just start and the first level of starting to change is understanding your emotions which I'm talking about now.

So, as I said there-was a group of people that were chained to the wall and could only see their shadows on the wall. After like a really long time one of them breaks the chains and escapes the cave. For our sake and Plato's, I will call this guy Jeff because I'm out of names.

So, before, Jeff and his friends thought that their whole reality was the wall of a cave and their shadows because they hadn't ever experienced or thought about the possibility of another reality and then one day Jeff manages to break the chains and escape the cave and when he comes out a whole new world popped right in front of him. It took him a couple of seconds to get his eyes used to the light because he had never seen sunlight in his whole life, all he had ever seen was darkness and his shadows made by the flames' light.

Then he felt extremely shocked because what once was his whole reality which was his own shadows had changed. His whole expectation of reality changed. He realized this turned into this whole new world with actual real-life colors, lots of green plants and even the blue sky itself and the bright and yellow sun. He was extremely surprised because what he once thought was reality was just an undeveloped illusion and now, he knew there is much more to reality than just shadows.

He himself realized that literally, his whole life had been a lie because this was the true reality so, with lots of excitements, he goes back to his friends to tell them about this new reality he has discovered and how there is a way bigger reality out there. So when he arrives to tell his friends, he is expecting them to be really surprised and eager to join him into this bigger reality, but when Jeff shared his experience on this new reality, they said that he is crazy and nuts and they told him that this shadow reality is the maximum reality because we haven't seen a more advanced reality than this. He decides to stay with his friends because he gives in that it was probably not real. So, I told you this story to show you our society's fixation on failures. Close to everybody think that failure is a bad thing, it's a negative thing, but this idea is kind of like the wall and the shadows.

This is our fixation on failure, and I don't know when maybe in the early future or late future humans will start realizing that failures are indeed good for us. In some sort of way, the idea of failure being a positive thing is the higher reality or like the more realistic reality and in my opinion Jeff's friends are like average people, they are fixed on one reality, one idea or even one fixation or one perspective and at the end you saw that Jeff didn't leave for that higher reality because he thought these two are doing this and it's probably better if I do it and he went along with the crowd.

Now, you might have realized that he went and joined the group of average people and I said this because I don't encourage you doing this. If everyone was supposed to be like the average than right now, we would not live in a world with so much technology because technology was made when some people decided they were going to do something new, when they decided they would not be like the average person anymore otherwise we would still be running around with horses and we would be eating ice cream with forks.

Thomas Edison, the man, the myth, the legend, got called "too stupid to learn anything" by his teacher and got homeschooled. He became one of the most influential inventors of our times and not with a happy and fine story. One of his quotes says "I have not failed. I've just found 10,000 ways that won't work." This literally means he tried to make the light bulb 10000 times and each failure was his mentor and thought him a way that didn't work, you've gotta respect that.

When Alexander Graham Bell was struggling to make the telephone, its owners got tired and offered all the rights of the product Western Union for $100,000. The offer was disdainfully rejected with the pronouncement, "What use could this company make of an electrical toy." In high school, actor and comedian Robin Williams was voted "Least Likely to Succeed." DO I NEED TO KEEP ON GOING? These people fought through and learned from all of their failures and in the end succeeded. They never gave up on their dreams and people still to this day benefit from their works. Not trying to do anything in life because you're afraid of failure and thinking that failure is a bad thing is something and the average/cowards achieve nothing.

As I said in my last book, don't be like the average because being average is boring lame and it won't get you any success and even right now, I still believe that there are ideas waiting to be discovered by other people. I said this because some people think that all ideas have been taken, all roles have been taken and there is no other idea or position in the world. You just must put your creativity and imagination into maximum overdrive. You can always develop a new strategy to goals you have in life and even in business and technology, you always think that ideas have already been taken but they have not, new things are developed every second.

We will talk about how fear disables creativity and our ability to take risks which are both vital for a successful path in any area you take in life. Failure takes courage and creativity takes authenticity, add those up and you've got success. The conversation has gotten interesting, so let's dive deeper.

So, believe it or not a top secret I have almost written two other whole books that I haven't published yet. Yes, that is right but they're not what you think. So, the first one I tried to write was my own life/diary about how I ended up coming to Canada and yeah it was pretty interesting. I wrote about 60 pages and the first 60 pages I was like yeah; I really like this it's awesome, I'm going to finish this, no problem and then after 60 pages I got demotivated because I ran out of ideas and I was like I can't do this anymore. Now, you have to consider that I was 8 years old at the time and I didn't really think I was going to be an actual author and be a New York Times' bestseller author (btw I'm not but I know I'm gonna be) that just goes to show you how much self-confidence and discipline I have. So yeah you could say I failed or quit but yeah, I gave up on it because I didn't really see any potential in it. That's the thing with humans, we are really passive beings you could say. Well, an even better description is that we're impatient, because we're in a convenient world where everything is on demand if you're willing to pay with money. You could get amazon prime (no adds btw XD) and your package could arrive in about 2 days which is super convenient, but as I said you have to pay to get convenience. You could go to Walmart and get the newest pc right there and then and bring it home and it

Beast Mode

set it up. so, to clarify if you pay for anything in this world you will get instant convenience, but there are some things that do not get achieved by instant convenience, but through hard work and integrity.

But humans do not respect that, they need to have that instant convenience, so they don't need to work hard and step out of their comfort zones. The only way humans can evolve and go into that next level of evolution is when they decide to be much more than they're limited to be and let's face it to do really seemingly awkward stuff like public speaking or trying to be yourself let's make an example. Ok so my example is that I myself play guitar and one day I was singing Havana by Camila Cabello, I like her music and then other boys are like ' ' (as they face palm) oh Shervin why do you listen to Havana, that's a horrible song like I like her music. Music itself is my personality, if I act so that I have to like music that other people like, I am not staying true to my personality and characteristics so I'm not being myself. That's the problem with today's society, with teens you should always be yourself because that's the only thing that's going to make you truly happy in your life because when you do something that you are forced to and don't like, it's not fun and that's what not being yourself feels like. So, if I like a certain type of music nobody is allowed to tell me to listen to another type of music unless it's a suggestion.

So, for some people, acting has become a daily habit, so now, they're stepping out of the box is trying to be themselves.

Back to stepping out of your comfort zone, I myself am a 14-year-old which means I have no responsibilities in life except doing my homework other than that, I can chill, play video games you know! Although I do those stuff almost every day, I still put some time for my personal career which also going to help me a lot, to an average person I'm doing extra work and putting more pressure in my life, but I'm actually putting myself over the limits which by itself has evolved me in life not only on a success level but on a knowledge level.

You have no idea how hard it is to do this and I'm not even bragging I'm just saying for an individual to evolve and be successful they need to step out of their comfort zone. And also one bad feature which is that all humans see is now, that's all they see they never try to see the future, like if I start doing this now, I will get results in the future, but no humans are not patient at all, we're always like what's in it for me. Let me make a flashback to when I said putting yourself out of your comfort zone another example by my first book (my diary from my last years in Iran until I came to Canada) I was afraid to finish it because I thought to myself that if I write this no one will read it because an 8-year-old kid wrote I and you know negative stuff so I quit on that. I wrote it on paper, and it's pretty cringy compared to my writing now, but you have to consider that it was the first thing that started it all. I still have it but if the public shows enough interest I can either mention it in my next book or I can rewrite it. So anyway, a year passes. I finished 4th grade and I moved from Moncton to Abbotsford, which is a gigantic leap from New Brunswick to British Columbia. I'm 9, so as all kids get dumb ideas, one day I get this idea of a superhero book, that's right, a superhero book called element man and no it's not avatar the last Airbender, god I get so annoyed when people ask me that. It's a superhero version of avatar (it was actually an avatar rip off).

I actually really enjoyed writing it, just extremely awesome characters. So fun fact one of my supervillain's names was a live man and if you're wondering what his superpower was. He can make anything he wants alive. So like metal, wood anything. I know it sounds dumb, but it sounded pretty cool in my head!

Yeah, so it was awesome, the momentum was good. I actually finished it and was thinking about making a sequel, but since I was a boomer, I had written it on paper, so me and my dad had to sit in my room every day and I used to read chapter by chapter and he had to type it, because fun fact he also had to check my English. He couldn't read my writing because it was messy and still is which is sad because I'm an author but whatever.

The reason I gave up on this one was literally everything. First, , I didn't feel like reading my own book every day, second, my dad didn't have enough time, third, I felt like I hadn't described the action scenes well enough and to be honest it was pretty hard, fourth, I thought it was cringy and would not be successful enough. Again, if the public shows interest I can maybe rework on it but its scraped for now. So anyway, you could say that I gave up and you might say in a sassy tone "but Shervin, in your last book you said to never give up on our dreams and to pursue and follow them". Yes I did quit, but the important thing is that I didn't give up because after I failed on those two books I started working on my third book because I saw a potential, so what I actually did is the first two times I got huge lessons for writing and then my third book which was dare to dream turned out super great.

So, I learned lessons from my failures. Now, if I would have published those first crappy books I would have never learned from my mistakes and I would have continued to be lazy and impulsive with my writing which is not what I like.

Failure showed me the mistakes I made in my writing so I could improve on my writing and be better at what I love doing the most and it also builds up your character to be a stronger person and not let things get to you. It's like this, fail more learn more and that's also another reason failure is good for you. Now, of course too much of anything is bad and if you're failing a lot it means that you're either not focused enough on your goal or you have little discipline in it or bad luck but that's very rare. I guess to conclude this section is this quote by the Pitbull

"There is no losing only winning, there is no failure only opportunities, there is no problems, only solutions"

Pitbull

This quote literally concludes what I'm trying to share with you guys in this book. First, it teaches you to be optimistic, like look how he doesn't say the negative but he said the positive which means every situation has a good side to it, even a negative one. One of my philosophies in life is to always be positive because as I said before life is a game and it doesn't really matter unless you want to torture yourself, you should just see the positive side to everything and acknowledge the negative but don't embrace it as you will become miserable.

No batteries for your Xbox controller? Too bad!

Which brings me to another quote that again I know isn't better than mine (sarcasm) which is by Bill Gates and it says:

"If you are born poor it's not your fault, but if you die poor it is your fault".

This quote just shows that your current circumstance is not permanent but if you keep on blaming others and not doing what's right which is starting a change in your life with your own determination and consistency than yes, your current circumstance is permanent.

Not only is poor but every other circumstance like not being satisfied enough with your grades or anxiety and depression. Why do you think some people drink alcohol and smoke cigarettes or do drugs, in my opinion, the first reason is poor parenting which is not your fault, it's not the parents' fault either because they learned all of that and their choice-making from their previous generation, guess you could say it's kind of the way it is, but parents should understand that they need to talk with their children and talk to them more about their own personal experience. Whether if its past or present and teach them the difference between right and wrong and also kids themselves should realize that they need to talk to their parents, like ask them questions more or even talk to them more about their normal life.

Beast Mode

When I see children with poor communication with their parents, I get confused and cringe because I start to compare my communication with my parents and the other person's communication with their parents and it's just weird like why would you not talk to them or even when it comes to making important decisions.

It really annoys me when people at our age think they're mature enough to make some important decisions, but clearly, they can't, they need their parents to help, because after all they have way more experience than you (about triple yours). The second reason some people rely on alcohol and etc. is poor emotional management which inspires all our actions and that is what I'm trying to teach in this whole section. If you think that parents should teach their kids about proper emotion management, you are correct, but it also relies a lot on personal experience as well.

It's kind of like biking, you have to experience it, you can't learn it by word of mouth, but you should read this whole section and then go talk to your parents about managing emotions. So back to our main topic which is about circumstances. If you remember, I told you that you have to give it time and also at that time think about some possible solutions. And a bunch of you might say that it is impossible and that my current circumstance is unchangeable but trust me you'll find it and I and you will be on this long journey to help each other out on this long journey.

Your parents can talk it out with you and solve your problem and make you happy. But there are also some things that cannot be changed, and you have to kind of let it go because that's just the way it is like parents' divorce. With some things, you've just gotta let it go because time solves all of our problems and mood swings.

TEEN PROBLEMS

Teen problems, oh my oh my. I bet most of you were waiting just to read this part of the book. Teen problems are such a gigantic issue no matter where you go because teens are our future generation and people don't want our future generation to be screwed up but to be perfectly honest most teen problems aren't matters of a problem but more of a strategy because you need a strategy to fight then.

I think the only very miniature amount of teen problems are unsolvable and need professional help. There is always a solution to everything, it just takes time and that's the main thing that I will touch on a lot in each of these problems. However, I really advise that even if you have none of these problems, that you read the description of the solution. Also, because these are really sensitive subjects, I researched a lot on the internet and also interviewed a lot of teachers that know a lot on teens, however, most of it will be my personal opinion.

However, I do have a unique perspective on mental health and mental issues because I'm from the Middle East and because I believe that the first step to becoming successful in life is having a free mind and that includes teen problems and teen mental problems and after you've fixed those, you can focus on your goals and dreams in life with a stable mind. Because if you go into your Beast Mode with a lot of problems in your personal life than you're going to run out of fuel fast and you'll no longer be able to continue your journey as a beast. So, yes, I do put mental health above everything else because that's the only thing that can stop me in life if it gets the opportunity to stab. So, yes, always make sure you're paying attention to your mental health because at this age we all think there is something wrong with us but it might just be because of our minds and this is why I find that it is necessary to discuss this and when you finally gain that mental freedom, that's when you're ready to become a beast.

The path to true freedom

"Care about people's approval, and you will always be their prisoner"

– Lao Tzu

What do you think is the feeling of true freedom? No, seriously, take a minute to question what the true feeling of freedom is. Because to understand the problem and the resolution, you've gotta see the ideal situation. It's when you know that you can do whatever you want without the fear of being judged.

Now, before I say one more thing, I would like to clarify that judging is fine because it's a personal opinion and you can't just tell people to stop judging because everybody has opinions but if they choose to share their opinion and it's wrong you have the power to shut them down. (This also goes for you, if you share your opinions be prepared to not be a sensitive person and suck it up.) In fact, I think it's perfectly fair to judge a person on their past deeds and not what they've done currently. I personally judge a person by their past deeds and what they've done, that helps me determine their intelligence and I will also judge them based on their interests but not too much because it's more of an opinion thing.

However as judgmental I am, I don't care if other people judge me because it doesn't really matter to me what they think, if I've done or said something bad I would like people to tell me but other than that if its fake criticism, I will debate with them because I love debating and I can't stand arrogant opinions that have no facts based upon them. So yes, judging is ok, its free speech but you shouldn't care about what other people think about you. So, it's basically a stalemate, everybody judges each other but also at the same time nobody cares. But what happens is when people care about what others think of them, it creates stress that shouldn't be there. I get called an idiot daily, you think I care, no because I have self-respect and don't really like to lower my value by overreacting and debating with idiots that waste my time. It just shows that you are so cheap that you're willing to waste your time with their immoral arguments.

Now, when I said what freedom really meant this is what I was getting into, living life on your terms, with your own beliefs and your own lifestyle without caring what anybody else thinks of you, that's what true freedom feels like. Maybe you like playing video games, like watching anime, baking whatever you like and being able to do those things without your conscience caring about the possibility of what others might think about it.

Finally transcending and being free from the social chains that everybody's tied you with and living life on your terms, when you want it and how you want it, that's what true freedom means, stopping caring about what others think. It really doesn't matter as I said earlier, when you do that, instantly a huge portion of your problems will be solved.

Beast Mode

And the main problem with caring comes down to this, we're so concerned about what others think of us we lose sight of what we are to ourselves. We forget our goals and dreams; we forget our hobbies and principles and we forget our values. So, while we make sure that others are comfortable, we lose our life values and meanings and fall into the abyss.

So, to clarify, I think that it is ok to judge but, it's not ok to be worrying about how others are judging you unless you've done something extremely bad and need to fix it.

And trust me, after you've made this decision in life, the feeling of freedom will be truly astonishing because most of the pressure that humans have on themselves is social pressure but when you just absolutely stop caring, you're free and others realize that they have to stop messing with you. Just don't get carried away and start being disrespectful and telling your parents I told you to do it because simply you just don't care. This also carries into when somebody's telling you how to do something or critiquing you on something, now, you're probably wondering how you can tell the difference when someone's just simply judging you and somebody wants to correct a mistake and the answer is that the two are easy to differentiate. Like sometimes you can tell if somebody is trying to correct you and improve you in that subject or just pure opinion judgment or they're just jealous. It's important because the right type of criticism can take us from being average to being absolutely astonishing.

As an example of being yourself and not caring, I have myself. I never change my personality so it suits somebody else more, some people like me and some people hate me and I don't care about the people that hate me and try to fix those relationships unless I had done something wrong and I actually care for the person enough to fix it. I have not, won't and will never change myself just to suit the haters better, I will always be honest with you, I will be a bit more logical than your mom that doesn't want to hurt your feeling and I will be weird and funny in a friendship. And it's not like I don't care but more like I stopped caring because I've cared so much in the past about what others think of me I felt numb and that stopped me from achieving my goals in life and just put a lot of stress and anxiety into my life but when I stopped caring it felt like morphine and everything felt nice and smooth.

But also, as with everything that I would advise you on, I will say the same thing, you need a healthy balance. Like if somebody comes up to you and talks trash to you about yourself and your goals and morals you should just ignore what they say because it's probably an area of life they're lacking in or an emotionally triggered response. But I guess it also comes down to your personality type, like me I'm more of a non-caring type

The transcendence to immortality

Now, can you guess what one reason that people worry about what other people think of them is? Just think about it for a minute, why would you care what other people think other than the fact that you don't have enough confidence in yourself and what you do.

And do you know where that comes from? It comes from not knowing yourself enough and not having discipline in what you do because if you do know yourself, you are willing to build up concentration on your interests and hobbies in life and in a term, those create your personality and that builds up your self-esteem and confidence. Now, since I've already talked about self-confidence, I'll leave that but what I haven't talked about which is really important are self-love and self-appreciation

So this could also be a helping hand for your problems, to start appreciating yourself and loving yourself more because the only person that will always be with you, take care of you and help you is yourself at every given moment and I might just make it sound easy but it's actually really hard but when you get it, your life will be easier when bigger challenges come.

"He who conquers himself is the mightiest warrior."

-Confucius

Since I'm alone for most times I just like to spend more time with myself and get to know myself more; we might all act as we know ourselves, but we don't. Even after being so alone I still don't know the full extent of my personality. You could say that I have a really weird personality as you'd say but I know a lot of my own habits because I really focus on what I impulsively do and try to fit in the other pieces of the puzzle and figure out my personality and set up plans for myself that suits my personality and if you're interested, I can describe my personality to you in a whole paragraph right now.

Here's my personality in a paragraph. I am extremely assertive and am not afraid to share what I think is true even if it might offend the other person, because I like to bring people out of their fantasies and bring them into their real-life selves even though it might be uncomfortable for them. But you know what, I say being uncomfortable with reality is better than being happy and delusional. In one of them you know you're not lying to yourself. This might cost me a relationship sometimes, but I'll be happy afterward because I like talking to real people than demented ones. This also brings me to my next statement which is that I really like to debate because I like to figure out the truth. This form of honesty can also enable me to be honest with my peers, so if I don't like somebody, I'll say it to their face instead of talking behind their back and making it a huge controversy because talking behind others people back is cowardly but confrontation isn't, if you have a problem with somebody as long as its justified, talk it out with the person.

One of the other things I like about my personality is that I don't care if some people like me or hate me, I will literally ignore them unless the relationship means something

Beast Mode

to me which in case I will try my best to fix the relationship but if somebody doesn't like me I'm not going to have depression like other people would I'd just be like screwing them, they probably aren't worthy and don't deserve my attention. I also love to spend time with my best friends because that's when I can feel the most myself and crack a few jokes. I also really like to be authentic in what I do because I'm really creative. I like to spend a lot of time by myself, whether it's homework or writing or playing video games, I feel really comfortable with myself.

I also have the habit of fixing problems myself instead of asking others a lot and have a lot of strategies to beat stress and anxiety itself because I spend a lot of time with myself so I know what types of strategies to develop. But to be perfectly honest I rarely feel anxiety and I think it's because I know myself so much, I've made this mental fortitude that nothing can really break. Lots of homework to do no stress, I'll just plan it out, somebody's blocked me on Instagram still no problem not everybody has to like you if they do that means you're trying to suit everybody. Besides I'm actually glad that person blocked me, I don't want to surround myself with negative people that will ruin my environment and atmosphere and they don't deserve me because my attention is something special to ruin. So yeah for me it's a process of elimination and the last people I like will become my friends because like currently I have like 4 really close friends because people who surround themselves with millions of people lack individuality and this cures their feeling of insecurity about themselves. I've spent so much time alone with myself that I've ensured total sanity and know myself inside and out because that's the entire point of life, rediscovering yourself, as I say it's the second birth.

If you can't write a paragraph about yourself as I did, then you have a serious problem in your life because it means you don't know yourself well enough and preemptively there is already a huge problem which will cause other mental problems.

Other than that, point what I really wanna focus on is to show you just how much spending time alone with yourself can help your mental health improvement in general. I have premade trust with myself that whatever happens, I'll be able to plan it out and solve it so the problems don't stagger.

This is why I basically never get mental problems unless there is something extremely wrong and I must change it and can't. This thinking will make you think at a helicopter view from all the thinking you do by yourself and not see the problem only in your view but from an outside view so you can compare them and get the best solution. This view also always reminds you that nothing is forever, even bad feelings. You got a bad test score and you failed the semester, school is really stressing because you maybe have some teachers that don't like you, you forget to do your own homework, one of your relatives died, these are all temporary problems and to be perfectly fair they do suck right now, but in the future it will all be ok, just ask yourself, will you feel the same in a month or a year. If the answer is no just to suck it up buttercup and take control of your life, remember that after a hurricane there is always a rainbow.

Beast Mode

This strategy of spending more time with yourself will also go with the type of people I hate because they're insecure and don't feel comfortable with themselves because they're weak. Of course, I'm talking about people who seek attention and no, I'm not talking about people who like to be the center of attention, those are more extroverted and outgoing people which is in their personality and they don't do it on purpose, they just like to communicate a lot.

What I'm talking about is people who are mentally insecure that they need 20 people in their friend circle to feel complete as a person, because alone they feel empty and try to change themselves so it suits others. Some people are even worse, to make themselves feel more special, they pretend to be the victim to get more attention. Like saying that the other person hates them in front of that person to get a reaction like "I don't hate you, we're best friends" or like for girls, when they post a picture of themselves and say that they're ugly, to await the 20 comments that say that they're not ugly and that they're pretty, so that they themselves feel better about themselves. The reason for that is because they have the expectation that others will say that they're not ugly, so they know that they're going to get comments and reactions that say that they're not ugly, but they just need that attention in the comment section and that confirmation from others, not themselves that they're not ugly. If that's not sad to you I don't know what is.

The thing I'm trying to get to that will solve a lot of problems instantly is that by spending time with yourself, you will enjoy your own presence. Just think about this, would you feel insecure if you were alone somewhere for 24 hours and had absolutely no contacts with anybody except yourself (not even texting). Of course, you would because you would get used to yourself and alone you would start seeing so many habits of yourself that you don't usually notice. I recommend that you do this at least for one day, it's truly an amazing experience. The reason spending time by yourself alone is important for the outside world is because success starts in the inner self and then shows its results on the outer side. If you can't handle yourself, then what can you handle in life? And the cherry on the icing is that you'll actually get goals done if you can stand yourself.

"Without great solitude no serious work is possible."

Pablo Picasso

You have to start to get to know yourself more, make a bigger bond with yourself, stop always hanging out with tons and tons of people just to make you made up loneliness and insecurity go away, instead spend more time with yourself and make that bond so your inner bond will be as strong as ever. For example, when I'm alone in the house, I treat myself to tea once a day and that makes me feel way better and I know it might sound crazy but I create a better bond with myself and this slowly makes my mental fortitude stronger so I don't get caught up in problems as easily.

When I watch a movie, I feel like I'm spending time with my inner self and that's another thing that makes my bond way better and when you make your bond better with yourself it helps you with things in life as I said previously.

When you spend more time with yourself, you also get more self-reflection time, on what you can improve on, you get more self-control and can handle your emotions before they handle you and you.

But let's just get something straight, I'm not saying be less social, I'm saying don't make big friend circles because you have a sense of insecurity. Instead of filling that insecurity by making a bigger friend circle (which comes from the lack of confidence) start spending more time with yourself, understanding yourself and trying to figure out what the hell is happening in your life while also increasing the bond between you and your personality instead of always hanging out with your 40 friends and never having a break. Friends are cool, but stop wasting your time with them all the time and sometimes spend time on what actually matters which is you. Try to see what part of this gigantic universe you belong to, try to figure yourself out, what your interests are, your goals and dreams and what your plans are that you will carry out and at the same time you will increase your bond with yourself which will help you with your emotions and mental fortitude.

Besides in economy when there is too much of something the value of it becomes less and the same goes for friendship, slowly they will all start losing their meanings and you can spend less time with each friend as you feel like a fork is scraping off of your soul.

You might think that of all the things I've said, that I'm actually an introvert, but the reality is that I'm actually an extrovert, that's why my overall communication skills and public speaking skills are good. I talk with everybody, but I rarely consider them one of my close friends because I have set a standard for myself of what I need out of a friend and most of the time it's that they can't be delusional, can't be dramatic, has to be smart and extremely honest, I have to like them. I basically consider very few my friends because I don't like to crowd my life with too many people. Does it mean I hate everybody? No, I like everybody except the ones that disrespect me but I just don't like having a huge friend circle.

I do act stupid and dumb in front of my friends because I like to make them laugh but they all know I have an intellectual side to things. However, when somebody disrespects me and it's not a criticism and they think that I'm my usual comical self and can't defend myself, like a straight-up insult, I will calmly and verbally dismantle them, especially when they're mad and think that swearing is a good idea to prove their points. I will calmly destroy them in a conversation just like attrition warfare which is a type of warfare that is really long but it slowly drains the enemy's resources and at some point, they will crumble. That's also another benefit of spending more time with yourself which I think I already said. I can manage my emotions easily, so if somebody comes at me angrily and says something random but offensive, hoping to get an angry reaction out of me and then after acting like the victim in front of other people, they instantly lose because I never react emotionally in an argument, because I have realized by myself that you instantly lose the moral fight. The moral fight is a sort of mental warfare that is given to the person that is the least disrespectful and who's trying to actually solve the problem. And the best part is that when people hate me, it's usually because I'm too honest with them. I've also developed myself so much in my free time when I'm alone that I can almost always control and handle any situation and that by itself is a really big advantage you can have over others.

Anyway we got off topic a bit there, as I said before, does me not considering everybody my friend mean I don't like them, no, I just don't want to expand my social circle so that it's out of hand and let everybody into my life because first, that's a waste of time and second, read what I previously said and also because I don't have any insecurities to cover with that.

The last paragraph shows the benefits of spending more time with yourself and to not overpopulate yourself but there's also another reason. It is that you can make standards, morals, and philosophies for your own life. So, for example, one of my morals and standards in life is that I demand respect by the way I talk which makes people respect me. When I want to get respect, I will speak with my intellectual side that everybody outside of my friendzone knows me for.

So basically, what I mean by morals and philosophy is what is your life view is gonna be like, what types of strategies you're gonna use, how are you going to judge people. For example, one rule I have is that I absolutely despise people who use drugs and marijuana other than justified medical use because I just think that they're stupid losers that have no hands because they can't type stress relieving tactics into Google and get some, so they just think that going to drugs is the next best way to relieve stress. I also despise them because I think they also do this to get more attention, like look at how cool I am,

I'm so different from other people because their parents never taught them the difference between right and wrong when they were kids.

I also despise people who defend celebrities that use drugs for stress relief, like they have too much pressure in their life. Oh, if you want to use that logic then why don't we turn into the busiest and the most pressured people in the world, businessman. In this case, let's use Jeff Bezos as an example, Amazon's CEO, the richest man in the world currently sitting at 137.6 billion dollars, now, can you imagine how busy the everyday life of Jeff Bezos is, how much pressure he has to endure every single day. Certainly, more than the celebrity. Now, if Jeff Bezos is going to live his life with the same ideology like the celebrities for stress relief, he'd be dead right now, from all the overdoses that would have happened to him. Do you want to know why, because Jeff Bezos is a person with proven integrity and has actually worked hard to get to where he is now and when you work really hard on a passion, you slowly become wiser and start valuing life and realize that you're not relieving stress but just digging your own grave.

They are smart and realize that drugs are really stupid. And this goes for everything, because celebrities instantly become successful and popular and work hard initially but then at some point instantly become famous, unlike businessmen who sacrifice everything on their work and realize the value life has, that's why I said they have more integrity than most of the celebrities who use drugs, because by working so much they've learned a lot of values in life step by step, they finally became successful. now imagine skipping all of that and instantly becoming popular, you wouldn't appreciate it just because you didn't work hard enough for it. So, from the pressure of all the money, they turn to drugs like cowards.

Now, why am I talking about this, I'm just showing you what one of my morals look like so you can develop one of your own when you're spending time with yourself. So, in a lot of social issues you can follow your morals and philosophies but just remember, don't be too stuck with the same morals all the time, be flexible for your morals to grow because flexibility is the only way we grow and become wiser by exploring different ideas and covering the possibilities of new options. Being enslaved by a philosophy, moral, ideology and political party is the lowest level you can go as a human.

Take care of yourself

"Self-care is how you take your power back."

– Lalah Delia

Now, spending more time with yourself also means paying more attention to your health and science has shown that if you pay more attention to your physical health it will also affect your mental health positively. So, if you have a lot of mental problems don't expect the stash of M&Ms to help your problems, and even though I love candy it sucks to say you can't eat it all the day and that you must add more organics to your daily diet.

Let me tell you why you need more organics because we basically become whatever we eat. Our body disposes the bad parts of the food and keeps the good stuff for your body, for new molecules in the body to be made. So literally you will become what you eat. With that in mind, it's probably better to add some fruits and veggies to your diet so you can just escape all the useless calories and actually help your body to have become made by better material.

Research has also shown that people who eat healthier have more energy in their overall day because they are eating whole foods instead of processed foods and this is interesting, because when you have more energy you can have a higher focus and attention level in your day, which in turn will lower possible mental problems you will have because you will have the energy to focus on your problems in life and also keep your head in school and at the same time you'll have a good social life.

Another way to a healthier lifestyle is by having a long sleep schedule. Recently a survey was done and it shows that teenagers sleep on average 7 hours even though 9 hours is the ideal time because sleep basically resets the body function and research has shown that, teens that get the proper amount of sleep have a better mood and are in term less likely to get mental problems because their body has more time to basically stabilize itself.

And the third thing you can do to take more care of yourself is to exercise because research has also shown that people who exercise more have a happier and healthier life compared to those who think that reaching out for the TV remote is a sin and who literally still play World of Warcraft in their mom's basement, are like 21 and not in shape. Also, another research has shown that when the body moves, it helps people who suffer from depression because when you're moving, you're basically getting out of your head and when your entire body is moving, your brain releases endorphins, one of the hormones that make us feel good. Anyway, if you follow these three steps, I'm pretty sure that your life will be free of anxiety and depression.

And this idea also goes with success and expectations, if you read this and already thought to yourself, man I can't do that, then how do you expect to achieve your goals and dreams in life, if you can't even make simple shifts in your habits so you can have a free mental state. This also goes with what I said earlier with schools and how they make kids feel special and how they tell students they can achieve anything they want just because they're special but they don't teach about how goals require patience and show you how you start small first and then slowly get big.

I'm going to make myself an offer I can't refuse

"Whoever is happy will make others happy."

- Anne Frank

This tip is also extremely important if you want to get rid of problems like anxiety stress and depression for the short term. For many people myself included, when we feel bad over a problem, we like to make ourselves feel good by doing what we like and that's really important because being in a bad mood really sucks and can put your life on hold and all your goals on pause because you're just in a bad mood and don't feel like doing anything. You should almost always do something that you like first in the face of a problem to get into a good mood and then try to solve it because you can't solve stuff on a bad mood. I'm just going to tell you some things that work for me when I'm not in a good mood so hopefully, you can get an idea for it.

So one of the things I do is I literally listen to music to calm myself down because music helps the brain to calm down and focus, it's been also shown in scientific studies that show that the brain likes music and calms down to the beat the music puts down, for me personally I like hip hop/rap artists because they just calmed my soul and make me concentrate on what I need to work on. When I come back from school, I sit at my computer, start Spotify and start doing my homework, especially with my book music really helps me to stay out of writer's block.

Another thing I like to do is Overwatch which is the best video game I've ever played and I like video games in general. I don't know why but whenever I seem to be having a problem or feeling choked up, I just put up Overwatch or League of Legends on my pc, pull up Spotify and play one of them with music. I don't know why but since I'm competitive when it matters the competitive nature of video games amuses and relaxes me. But overall, I don't care what I do as long as it makes me happy because that's what matters in the end. That's why we crave accomplishments and success in the first place, I mean of course you could argue that sometimes it might be for your parents' satisfaction but mostly it's for our own satisfaction, it drives that instinct of self-righteousness, that we're better than other people because we're more accomplished which sometimes can be correct if what you're doing is actually helping the society or community. This feeling is fine as long as it doesn't make you cocky and too overconfident because if you don't know how to manage confidence and cockiness than it can blind you and can make you do and say things that you will regret afterward.

Just remember this, when you're feeling bad always do something that makes you happy, not something that you're forced to because that doesn't make you happy, listen to music, take a walk, watch Netflix, I don't care what you do just make sure that your end result is happiness. After that when you're relaxed enough you can sit down and see what you can do about your problem. Life has many ups and downs but in reality we're all fighting for our happiness in this twisted, fake world that we're giving meaning to that really doesn't matter and when you realize that reality doesn't matter you will try your hardest to make yourself happy and forget the reality (that's why we adopt things like relationship and responsibilities into our lives instinctively because without those we had to face the fact that reality is boring and dull). That's why if I had the choice of being dumb or smart, I would choose dumb because dumb people have a really low understanding of reality and that gives them happy because they're stuck in their little worlds just like the majority of the teenagers. As you become smarter, you become more miserable because you realize that nothing matters and that by itself will be a midlife crisis for most uneducated teens when they grow up, so in a sense perhaps being stupid is a privilege in some sorts, you'll always be happy and your problems will be with people instead of ideologies.

Great minds discuss ideas; average minds discuss events; small minds discuss people

- Eleanor Roosevelt

This quote is perfectly an explanation of what my morals are in life if all you're ever talking about in life is useless and there is nothing productive going on than you will stay that way just like the decent adult I mentioned. At least if you've even realized that reality is pointless, you should still try to be the best version of yourself so you can have a challenge in life because challenges are another way of giving fake meaning to our boring and dull reality.

My problem isn't talking about other people, in fact, I sometimes talk about other people, I have no problem with gossiping, everybody gossips at least a little it's a form of natural communication, but I'm talking about the dramatic people who always talk about other people and their relationships, Instagram status and etc., but their lives themselves aren't even stable.

The reason I talk about entire subjects, philosophies, and ideologies is that every time I explore them, I learn something new that I hadn't before and that makes me really satisfied, knowledge drives me because being in Beast Mode also means being knowledgeable and wise.

Like I bet you the teenagers that talk about other people, like relationships, celebrities and gossiping have no idea what's going on around them. They don't know a thing about history, but hey they can tell you the exact dating history of everyone around them which is absolutely useless and provides no information. I bet you they have never picked up a good book, video or article in their lives and basically have no knowledge of their own. So please don't be that teen that just wastes all their time on talking about other people, focus on your own life and become smarter instead of being dramatic.

The problem with today's world as meaningless as it is is there are too many inconsistent adults in society and those are basically the dramatic people I was talking about during their teens. Not learning anything and stopping learning is a sin because we want more confident and stronger adults in society and you're the future generation and we need smart people for the future generation, not a bunch of people that think watching high school musical was the biggest highlight of their life and having unsuccessful lives who contribute nothing to society.

Difference between true happiness and being high

"Happiness is the meaning and the purpose of life, the whole aim, and end of human existence."

-Aristotle

There are two types of happiness, moral happiness and temporary happiness and oh boy, are these two different.

Temporary happiness: Temporary happiness is just like getting high, smoking cigarettes or drinking and being happy, it's temporary, it will not solve your life eternally but it sure will make you feel good for now. You might feel as if heaven has been brought down from the sky to the ground but it really hasn't. The reason I brought this subject after the previous chapter about doing things you like is that sometimes, we confuse temporary happiness and moral happiness and we think that our problems could be fixed with just always having temporary happiness.

Sometimes you could get it mixed up with real happiness. Now, I'm going to use myself as an example, in grade 7 I was part of the play my school was doing because we were doing Lion King and you might think that I feel really overconfident and too arrogant and will turn down small opportunities but no I like having overall small experiences in life because you learn something from all forms of experience, even small ones. So, in the play, I got the role of an elephant leg and it was pretty fun, to be honest, and also because we got to miss the school for about a week and there was no way I was missing that. Now, at the same time I was doing rugby and the play practices were ruining my rugby practices and the thing was that the play practices were going to go on for like three weeks, and we had the rugby practices for one month. Which meant after three weeks I would have only had one week of practice for rugby before the season started and I didn't want that because you will literally get stomped when you have no idea what to do in rugby.

So, I was stuck between having to do the play and not do rugby because there was no way I would enter the season with one week of practice or quit the play and stick to rugby. This was a real fork and you know when you are pinned or forked in a situation, you don't really know what to do so you start just forgetting the situation because you know it's the easy way out. Running at your problems head-on is the hardest choice a person can make.

So anyway, an example of temporary happiness would be to just try to make distractions to forget your problems like watching Netflix, playing video games and etc. But here's what happened, I finally sat down with Mr. Lilly and we talked it out like grown adults, but I ended up quitting rugby because it was not a part of my personal interest to enter the season with weak experience. But yes, what I want to get to is that even though distractions might give you temporary happiness, it won't solve the problem and it won't give you moral happiness. I guess now's the right time to introduce moral happiness.

Moral happiness: When you feel happy eternally from either solving a problem or achieving the goals you so desire. Another example, many adults will tell you that their lives are fine but the part they won't tell you is that they don't have moral happiness. Now, this could either be from not a good partner choice (which is the schools and parents fault) It could be financially or even just that they didn't achieve the goals they desired as a childhood and now, they're just like all the other decent adults in society that live paycheck to paycheck with nothing to eat but sardines.

So, they will tell you they're fine but inside they don't have moral happiness and they either find a hobby or distraction so they don't get reminded that they are morally not happy and are suffering whether if they show it or not and they will keep that feeling until their death. Or maybe they stacked their problems up and now, it's a gigantic mountain for them to climb because they didn't take responsibility for them sooner.

Now, let's get simpler again, in that situation with the play, if I would've just let the due date come and just distracted myself with video games, so I could gain temporary happiness and ignore my responsibilities, the problem would just suddenly slap me in the face because moral happiness has caught up to me and it's asking me what the hell were you doing in those three weeks. This also happens with adults but in that case its long years that they weren't aware of their lives, it's called a midlife crisis. Moral happiness just starts asking you what the hell have you been doing your entire life, just avoiding responsibility for the comfort of temporary happiness?

So just remember I said that when you have a problem do things that make you feel happy but, just remember don't get too stuck up in it because you will feel the temporary happiness by the distraction but not the moral happiness and when you come back to face reality, all of your responsibilities will be staring you in your face. We are always aware of the problem that separates us from moral happiness but we don't like to remind ourselves to do it until it's too late because the mind knows that whenever you focus on moral happiness it feels lazy to do anything actually productive to finish that goal and get that moral happiness, whether it's achieving a goal or solving a problem, so we try to avoid it until the due date, whenever that may be. You should run straight to your problems fearlessly, try to solve the problems and not try to avoid it because if you don't, that problem could catch up to you and be even a bigger problem at that point and all the meanwhile you will not have moral happiness. After running towards the problem and solving it then you will achieve mortal happiness.

Facing your problems is a good habit to get into as you become an adult because in adulthood you will have a lot of deeper problems. So, for my example, I had that conversation with Mr. Lilly. Solutions to problems could sometimes be difficult to do, but trust me, doing it will make you feel way better afterward and in turn you will feel way more moral happiness. And even better, the cherry on the icing is that you learn to handle responsibilities which in my opinion is the single most important skill to have.

Change what you can

Which is what I'm slowly getting to. One of the greatest people I usually listen to daily to expand my knowledge is Dr. Jordan Peterson who is a clinical psychologist that used to teach at Harvard and the University of Toronto. But he's more than just your normal psychologist and teacher, he is one of the smartest people I've ever seen and gives priceless advice on life that leaves my jaw dropping for what it would seem like an eternity and that's why I watch his videos daily.

He advocates a lot for young men losing their gender expression and confidence because he says what I said earlier which is, modern schools are stripping away what makes boys become real men.

I will tell you one of his best tips for increasing your competence and approaching the world with your goals and dreams from personal experience as a teenager, I can tell you, you should take this Dr. Peterson's tip seriously because he himself has made me feel very motivated and empowered as a teen and what it means to be a real man and a human being.

One of his ideas was on basically young people in the modern day coming out of universities and colleges feeling all mighty and special because their schools and parents taught them so and they think they have politics and economy figured out and they think they can change the world, so then they become activists and do useless protests.

Beast Mode

What Jordan Peterson was talking about in his Joe Rogan podcast and many other ones was that instead of doing useless protests, first clean your room because your room is kind of a definition of who you are as a person and when you clean your room, you're building competence in yourself. Another amazing theory he has taught me is that each time you take the steps that you know you should but most times you wouldn't, you build integrity and doing the right thing and slowly build your confidence, integrity, and self-esteem. These will all grow and then you can change the world after a long time of experience.

It's a very simple feeling, like you know you should clean your room, but you wouldn't because you're lazy. What Jordan Peterson says is that some people want to change the world but they can't even start off by cleaning their own room because they're lazy, so what he says and I absolutely love this, is "If you can't clean your room, then who the hell are you to tell the world how they're supposed to live?"

This is actually a pretty intelligent quote when you think about it because when you start doing what you know that you should be doing and not being lazy, in time you will develop this integrity like feeling in yourself because with each action you take over the things you know you should do and when you do those your competence builds up and slowly you can change the world instead of immediately being delusional and thinking you can change the world.

Cleaning your room basically means that you're basically progressing as a person and you're doing what is against the favor of what your mind wants to do which is sitting around and do nothing and by going against that, you develop your competence and discipline.

Then after that's done you go "hey maybe I should practice the guitar more instead of sitting around the TV all day and doing absolutely nothing" which is what your mind tells you because here's the thing we all have moral obligations, we know we all must gain accomplishments to make our parents proud, we all know that we should have a healthier lifestyle, we all know we shouldn't lie to ourselves but we don't do it because we're lazy.

If we do what we feel is morally right to do, then we'll just build so much more competence, because you'll know that you're always doing the right thing and that just turns on a trigger in your head that if doing your moral obligations feels good and gives you more competence and confidence, then it will eventually give you a good outcome in life. That way you do more moral obligations you feel condemned to but are locked up by the chains of laziness like "hey, what if I practiced my guitar more" or "what if I improved my relationship with my parents so that when hard times come, they will help me." I mean they should do that instinctively but it's still good to develop a good relationship with your parents by yourself, if they won't. Then you do those and slowly you build up like "hey I should enter America's Got Talent to increase my popularity" and then you get to more critical life choices as an adult like choosing the person you know will stand by you in marriage "should I propose to this person whom I will be condemned to for the rest of my life" and breaking relationships that you know won't work. Eventually, by doing what's right you will end up achieving success based on your own definitions for it.

So yes, it's a good habit to get into because it gives you more competency to challenge yourself more in life and keep on increasing your level of goal achieving and eventually if you're lucky enough, you can change the world when you've reached that god-level competency.

And this is also another way you could create that bond with yourself. By doing what you know you should do but won't do. When you're going against laziness, that creates the sense that you're allied with your inner self which always wants the best for you. After that you both against the resilience which is the laziness and that confidence booster you get which is a form of trust in yourself will improve your mental fortitude because your mind will figure out that you've done nothing wrong and that you're consistently honest and basically that sense of innocence makes your relationship with yourself way better.

For example, Michael Phelps is the best swimmer to have ever lived. He has said that he practiced 6 hours a day when the other swimmers barely practiced half of that. He said that since he was a child, he always wanted to be an Olympic swimmer, and do you know how he accomplished that? By doing what he knew he was supposed to do, which for him was practicing 6 hours a day to reach that level of swimming he always wanted. And trust me by doing his moral obligations which were practicing hard to achieve his dreams he achieved his dreams and even surpassed them. Even if he failed, he would still be a happy person because he knew he gave his best and it is what it is and that happiness is what everybody should look for because it will definitely make your life better.

This tactic of Dr. Jordan Peterson is so good that other than the fact that it increases your bond with yourself and that it helps you increase your mental fortitude, it can also help you with a lot of your mental problems such as depression because usually in depression you feel like you're cornered from every direction, nothing matters and everything feels hostile. At times you might feel that it's your fault because of like what happened, cause your depression tells you that you're guilty but when you do what you know you should and are supposed to do, you gain more integrity.

Then when you get more integrity, you'll know that you're a good and honest person that does what is needed and necessary and that feeling of innocence will counteract the feeling of guilt of when you did something wrong. That's why it's better to always do this so your mind can be self-conscious of the fact that you're an honest and innocent person, that does whatever they can to improve their life. so that basically you have these preemptive defenses set up for mental problems, so when they come after you, your mind already has defenses set up and has a strong fortitude like "Nah man it's not my fault, I'm an honest person, I'm not to blame here I always do the right thing that I know I'm supposed to do".

Now, obviously this is not an every time solution, some depressions are caused by a lot of stress and sometimes it's when you focus too much into reality and realize nothing matters, as I explained earlier, this ideology is basically nihilism which many people experience and it is basically when you realize nothing matters and everything is basically social constructs. And that social constructs are made up to reduce the suffering of reality by things like relationships, religion, and emotions, so your belief in those reduces your overall suffering from the truth that nothing really matters, that maybe even mental problems are not that serious after all.

As I've explained before, that feeling is horrible, when you know nothing matters, we're all going to die one day and you can't pause time, it just keeps on ticking like a spoon that's scraping off of your soul.

When you enter this zone you get an existential crisis which is the philosophical term for when you question if your life has any value whatsoever and if everything is as pale as it seems and if even living is worth it and after a while you fall into the abyss and it's really hard to get out.

Not going to explain too much because I think I've already explained enough in past paragraphs but essentially know that if you have this problem, you're not alone, I have gotten this problem a lot and have had a lot of emotional twists from it normally but what I can tell you is that you're lucky if you have this problem, because research has shown mostly intelligent people get existential crisis because they question reality more.

However, if it's a common occurrence it can become a big problem with your overall mood in general, what you do to solve it depends entirely unto you but what I do is I think of all the things I value in life even though life has no meaning, more of like an emotional response. I laugh a lot because even though I care for the responsibilities I choose to take care of in life and how serious I am to help teens, I seriously still don't care about it and I know that might sound weird but if you meet me in person you'd know what I mean. I'm a funny person in general and laugh a lot, one of the antidotes to meaninglessness is laughter.

My philosophy on life is that you should not care about life but at the same time you should try to create meaningful relationships because those are the things that look like they matter in life and the only thing you find real and my second philosophy in life is don't be stupid so you can make others happy. I know many teenagers like to waste their time but my tip for them is please don't be stupid for your whole life and try to always learn more because when you know more, that's what real competence, confidence, and power feels and with that you can make other people feel better so they can go out into the real world, grow their competence and help other people just like you. That's basically what I try to do,

That's another thing that I would say kind of matters. It's also another good way to have a better bond or relationship with yourself. As for everything else, my lack of conformity to traditional laws and modern norms has to show you I actually don't care about trends which also include rules because trends/rules are temporary and they limit the capacity of the amount of knowledge you can use and you realize that when you realize how big this universe is and how small humans are, you figure out how stupid norms and trends are. So that's why I don't like to follow modern norms and rules but just create my own extremely unique pathway in life and make others persuade me instead of me persuading and being enslaved to another modern norm and not learning. Like some people are

30 and you ask them what the hell have you learned about life in these 30 years and they can't answer you which is absolutely insane.

It all just comes down to the feeling of hopelessness in both philosophies I represented, doing what you know you should be doing and not doing things that will make you look weak, they attribute to hope. As I already stated, the reason humans keep on progressing in life is because of that hope we have. So the best way to beat an existential crisis or the realization of one's own meaningless, is to have hope, both of the philosophies I presented gave me more hope to continue life and you just must find your own philosophy within your life so you have a better life and a more motivated one.

Most feelings of existential crisis come from the feeling that you're not special, and that's true, nobody's special but you can be. Modern schools and parents like to shove this ideology that we're all special down our throats but I'm not your parents and I don't buy that crap. It's true we're all unique because we all have a different set of values but the uniqueness and being special are two different things and here's the deal, you might not be special, but I can see it in you, I can see it in everybody. Everybody's unique in their own ways, but special is different, you become special, and only very few go through that evolution.

The reason you're even reading this book is because you want to get in Beast Mode which means you're looking for improvements in your life, achieving all of your goals and having a strong mentality and feeling competent and confident (either that or your parents forced you to read this book). So even the fact that you picked this book shows you are willing to let change come into your life and let you grow. That means you're a progressive individual and want to succeed. Trust me with enough determination, discipline and great mentality that can keep you from wasting time (our most valuable resource) you should be able to consider yourself special. I can just see that in progressive people looking to get into the Beast Mode. So, to put it briefly, being special is not something you're born with but something that can be earned.

Tell the truth even though it might hurt

"Being entirely honest with oneself is a good exercise."

-Sigmund Freud

Hypocrisy is a natural human thing as we all engage in the art of human hypocrisy because we all have a certain mask that we're trying to hide. Hypocrites who are hypocrites on purpose are the cowards I was writing about at the beginning of the book, the people that feel too weak or insecure so they pretend they don't follow popular trends and norms so other people will see them as in the term of "cool" so that way they can make more friends by pretending to be unique (so basically looking for attention).

The worst thing about people who are hypocrites is that they're lying to themselves and that goes against what I was saying earlier about building your competence based on cleaning your room and always doing what you know is the right thing to do, so you make an honest and true form of yourself that you're not guilty of. If you practice this daily then you'll have less mental problems, because by facing what hurts and into uncharted territory which in this case is the truth and that is also another way to build your mental fortitude, other than spending more time with yourself.

I guess what we should really talk about then is the rise of hypocrisy in the modern generations and how it makes society more vulnerable to extreme sensitivity. What I always like to do to simplify even the most complicated problems in my life is to define my terms so I can break down the problems to simpler meanings so let's get hypocrisy right. What's the antonym to hypocrisy, to me its honesty and I think that most people can agree on that definition as well? So, I basically realized that when I came from Iran is that Westerners are too sensitive and I did not understand why and as I developed my political knowledge, I understood the correlation between society and politics and how those two interact.

I feel as if as time passes, Western civilizations are becoming more hypocritical because honesty, the antonym of hypocrisy is becoming less and less while emotions and the sense of oppression in people is increasing at the same time. They compare utopia with the real world and as a conclusion they lose their intimate relationship and honesty within themselves.

Right off the top of my head I can tell you another reason the sense of oppression and feeling of victimization is increasing, because these cowards I was describing are coming out into the real world and they have this ideology where if they don't succeed they blame the system or don't have a 6 figure income and think there is something wrong with everything and are basically narcissists because they blame everything on others and the system that created it but what they are not self-conscious about is their own lack of discipline that can't achieve them anything in their lives.

Again, I think this is a habit that schools teach children by making them narcissistic and telling them they can achieve anything they can. So what happens is they become delusional as they get older because when you're living in a lie you're considered delusional and what I'm going to teach you in this chapter is how to not be delusional and lie to yourself, so you can be more responsible in your personal life and feel less weak mentally and build up your personal integrity and competence by being truthful to yourself. Don't lie to yourself, because it makes you delusional, don't be delusional because your life becomes fake, don't live a fake life because a fake life is not worth living. So, first, let's talk about the first most hypocritical/dishonest thing you can possibly do for yourself, victimization.

So, you might be confused by what this means, and what I mean by this is that when people act offended or like the victim to get more attention. Now, the reason that I'm including this in the help section is that victimization makes you feel weak and that leaves you vulnerable to mental problems.

Just remember, the one thing you take out of this book should be, prevent yourself from feeling weak and live with integrity by doing what you know you should be doing like Michael Phelps so you adopt a form of responsibility in life, that gives your life meaning. Let me elaborate and give some examples, making yourself feel weak essentially comes on the fact that when you know there's something you shouldn't do because at the results it will make you feel weaker morally, just like how cleaning your room and doing the right things when they matter increases your competence, this habit of doing things you know will make you feel weak will make you lose all hope and confidence you had before this. It makes you feel weaker not only in front of other people but to yourself which is even worse because when you lose the game of life from the inside, that's when things become harsh and dull on the outside.

For example, I'm going to use a social media example. When you request to follow somebody on Instagram and know that you will get rejected, because you don't have a good relationship with them but for the sake of the small chance to get accepted you do it anyways. Then you come back the next day on Instagram and see that on the person's profile the follow button is blue again and it says follow which obviously means you got rejected, that action you just took made you weaker. You feel like your moral self has gotten crushed because it's becoming weak and you blame yourself for the stupid thing you have done, that you shouldn't have because now, you feel weak for doing the wrong thing.

Now, that's an example of a thing you know you shouldn't be doing because you will feel weak afterward. You know that the persons not going to accept your friend request but you will try anyway because for the small percentage of hope they will accept and that it will be happily ever after and meanwhile the majority of your brain is measuring how much of a catastrophe it would be if you can't get that relationship back anymore and you think that something's wrong with yourself and this goes for majority of social media. Not just requests. Like how people check their followers every day and check to see who unfollowed and like why aren't my number of likes going up? Is there something wrong with me? Do they not like me anymore? Like what is wrong with us and I know some of you might be like don't insult teens, but I legitimately consider that if you see your entire life value through a social media account and nothing else then you're just legitimately insane and your life is sad.

We need the good old days back where when you screwed up, the wildlife set you straight. Again, I don't know why schools don't teach modern teens useful advice instead of I don't know Pythagorean theorem. But anyway, let's get back to my original points, it's our hope to revive that relationship that makes us do it but at the same time we have the fear of that if we get rejected to that original estate which all humans are, which is loneliness will make us lose tons of hope so we get stuck. So, in a way, the rejection will make every human realize how lonely they are and whether people agree or not we're all afraid of that feeling on the inside.

What I said earlier also relates to this which was making that bond with yourself and building that mental fortitude so you don't really get shaken about simple problems like this one or loneliness. Let's look at another problem that I see with people but mostly drama queens do all the time. That is looking for attention while they pretend they are being offended, harassed or even weak. So, they find the perfect opportunities to look for attention in conversations where the other person could be easily misinterpreted.

This is one of the lowest standards you can hit, and it will just morally obliterate you because of the dishonesty that you're feeding yourself and you become delusional. You become an extremely mentally weak person. Don't feed yourself lies, you'll become delusional, don't look for attention, you'll become weak, don't listen to what others have to say, you'll give up. Part of the, what you know you should do and don't do what will make you weak is also the public image concepts. So, if you for example act oppressed for attention, others will easily see through that and understand that you're a morally weak person and will want to have fewer interactions with you because they know that whenever they have that interaction, you will just produce a soap opera drama.

Now, some people take enjoyment out of victimization and use it in an acceptable way, I'm thinking like girls that pretend they're ugly just for others to comment on how pretty they themselves are and this has no downsides because girls enjoy it for whatever reason but it's a bad habit to get into especially as you grow up, because it affects your character. You don't want your character to be needy for attention and desperate for positive comments and when you do that, probably, nobody's gonna give a damn because they all want to get some money and eat some sardines so they don't starve to death. That's how the world works, every man for himself

So, here's my basic summary, be absolutely honest with yourself so you will become more strong, competent and have more integrity and let me tell you staying honest and true to yourself will be really good for your current problems and for your future as an adult. We need more dominant adults and those are adults who are honest to themselves and others who consistently take actions not to make themselves weak but to make themselves more competent and confident until they get to a point where they can contribute to society in some way, that's the types of people we need and you'll be one if you live your life honestly with yourself.

Cha Cha Cha Cha Changes!

Speaking of truth, let's come to one truth you must accept sooner or later in life. First, Shrek 2 is the best one in the series. The second thing is that change is a part of nature, change happens to animals, plants, etc. Change is mostly good because each time something changes, we analyze it and judge if it's good or bad and as a child that's where we learn to differentiate good and bad and it's essential to our survival.

But with change, there is also a feeling of insecurity that we don't have control over things. The desperation and the misery of the feeling you cannot fight against the change in life are mesmerizing and horrifying. An example would be when you're an adult and facing a divorce, you know you can't control your other partner and you must follow their wishes if the situation is that you want to stay in the marriage but they don't, you know the change is that you will be divorced and you can't fight against the change, that's the feeling of insecurity that change brings, it's the feeling of inevitability that will get you in depression because reality's gonna run over you like a bulldozer.

The sooner you face that change is inevitable and you can't control everything, you gain yet another way to eternal happiness. The feeling of not having any control is actually the most control you will ever have in your life because you'll know what to do after that feeling of starting from 0 and this is another way of avoiding a midlife crisis (depression).

Humans have a feeling of security when they're children and think they can control everything and schools kept that mindset in check for them until they grew up and now, they become aware of even bigger problems and they still think that they have everything under control and when things go wrong and they fail at something, reality just hits them, they feel they didn't have everything under control and that they failed and after that well they fall into a big dark hole they can't get out of, filled with sadness, anger, and guilt.

However, if you understand that you don't have everything under control and that change will surpass you, that's when you feel really free because you actually know that you can't control somethings and you must deal with it. With my earlier example which was marriage, you can try to gain control and talk to your other partner about how you can figure it out like a normal person would instead of divorcing right away but there are just things you can't control and if you know you can't control them you will be happier trust me. Lose the feeling of control because a problems gonna come one day and screw up that feeling of control and hit you in the face and then the actual feeling you had no control whatsoever makes you feel worthless and weak and as you know I'm against that feeling in my Morals because it lowers your competence and confidence, so it's better to feel you have no control than having the illusion you have things under control but having your party ruined when reality catches up to you.

There are also some changes you shouldn't be upset about, like moving on from friends and making new ones because all your old friends wanted to do was make you feel down and feel bad and trust me it's really important to have good friends because they make up your environment and only in a good environment can you grow. A plant cannot grow without sunlight, it needs a good environment, so do people in order to grow. So yes, if you have people that constantly make you feel bad and tell you that you're not good enough, you will indefinitely fail and won't grow as a person. You want friends who empower you when you don't feel like doing it, not discourage you when you have legit accomplishments. You want people who genuinely care for you and feel happy about you and are with you both in the sad times and the happy times, the downs the lows, you want people you can trust. So, a relationship isn't working out, cool, just end it, saves time and gets you away from fake friends.

Peer pressure

"Don't you ever let a soul in the world tell you that you can't be exactly who you are."

-Lady Gaga

Now, Lady Gaga is one of my favorite singers and yes, her singing is absolutely amazing and not only her singing but just because of her personality. Usually, when people get famous, they give up who they are and become fake but Lady Gaga takes none of that. She somehow managed to keep her weird and amazing personality and still was able to be a celebrity with nobody changing her habits and simply not caring about what others think. When you've reached the level where you don't care about what others think you've reached a new level of freedom.

In an interview, she was talking about what it means for her to be yourself and she said that "you all have a lot of people around you that tell you what you have to do but it's your right to choose what you do and doesn't do." And I can't agree more with Lady Gaga here. It's like people have to act fake and agree to things that make them uncomfortable but suits others and you're just here wondering since when did self-priority stop, like why aren't I happy. Maybe you aren't happy because you're doing what pleases others while you're making yourself suffer, and as long as anybody suffers, they won't be happy.

With that comes to peer pressure and not the good type but the bad type which I previously described as giving you suffering. It is important too, first, indicate that peer pressure is not a simple problem because in each teen it's different because they all have different backgrounds, ethnicities, and circumstances and sometimes it can be an extremely difficult problem. As you see in this stage, humans are developing mentally and grow away from their parents because they want to become more independent because they're sick of their parents tracking their every move but they get more frustrated as they still rely on their parents for money, food, clothes, shelter and etc.

As they become more independent, they develop more desire for social values, and they practice those hard until they become more social and find friends. Now, to keep those friends sometimes they will face problems such as peer pressure which basically means that their friends will expect them to do something and the person doesn't feel comfortable with doing it. Then your entire mind is conflicted over what to choose and they will have anxiety for any consequences that their choice will make, in all of them the peer pressure comes from the fear of loneliness because you'll fear that if you reject the peer pressure than you'll lose that friend and will be left out and everything will become lonely and that's a scary feeling.

This is why I was also explaining that you need to make a better bond with yourself and have that mental fortitude because some things hit hard but nothing hits harder than life and when that happens what the hell are you gonna do, this is in my mind the simplest problem out of the many other problems you will face in your life. So, when you have the

Beast Mode

premade bond with yourself, even though the hardest of conditions you will stay though and won't break easily even loneliness, as absurd that it might sound, you will enjoy it.

The worst part of this is that the pressure might increase or decrease depending on who your friends with, because some might be stubborn and annoying, while some might be more relaxed and gentle and it's the ones that are hyperactive that can be the most annoying to get through. The calm friend is so calm they can defuse a nuke or like the thing you feel obligated and pressured to do with that friend is to go to your school's green tea club at lunchtime, I know that that's a horrible example but it correctly represents how calm this person is; you might feel obligated to drink or do drugs with the other more dangerous friend.

There are three possible solutions I will give you, one of them requires you to be brave, one of them requires you to be authentic and the last one requires you to be vulnerable.

First, say no, now, this goes when people straight up ask you to do something. I know that might sound like a thing that doesn't require you to be brave but you might be surprised how some teens choke and how hard confrontation itself is for them. It's easy for me because I'm a god of everything and have maximum self-confidence and have found the meaning of life but I can understand this might be really hard for mortals (sarcasm).

Now, not only is saying no, not only important for peer pressure but for general everyday life, if you can't stand up for what you're comfortable and your beliefs and standards in life then how do you expect others to stand up for you. Besides

Beast Mode

there will be other times in life there will be way more at stake than pressure, it might mean your job, marriage or even something serious, who knows? Life is full of unexpected turns. This also goes with what Dr. Peterson said earlier and how I compared the two. At times, there's an important decision that's at stake and if you take Dr. Peterson advice and you do what you know you should do then afterward that will make you feel more competent and sometimes that decision that will make you more competent would be saying no; this is another one of those scenarios. Let's just take an example that's common, the class clown. As the whole class is in the discussion about a book and it's a serious discussion, your friends signal you to make a random hilarious joke you had discussed with them and everybody was laughing their butts off.

Now, I know some of you might call me a hypocrite for saying that kids can't be creative in class but this is a different discussion, this is about individual choices. It comes down to what do you want your social reputation to be and what your mind tells you. If your motivation is to be the class clown than mission accomplished, because you want to see some happy faces that will laugh at your joke and you'd give the whole world to see those glittering laughing faces and entertain them in this boring discussion. If you do this then you'll get those laughs and will be the class clown and if that's what you want to be remembered by (social reputation). Now, we get to the second part of the decision making, your choice will be based on the two philosophies I presented, doing the things you know you should do but don't do because you're lazy, but if you actually do it you'll benefit from it because you'll be more competent after that (exp. making your bed). So in this case if you keep yourself from telling that joke than you'll have a higher competence level because you persisted from telling that joke that will be extremely hilarious and that requires a lot of effort, so your mind will send that alert to yourself that you're a better human, because you held yourself from interrupting the class and all these small decisions slowly will build up your competence.

And the second philosophy is to not do things that will make you feel weak. Now, again in this situation how much will you make yourself like a complete idiot and loser and feel like the weakest person in the room. Like you might think that you'll gain everybody's respect and be popular the next day, but they're just basically gonna see you so as an idiot and I know that I said that what other people think doesn't matter, but in this case it does. In a normal case people usually object you for doing something differently and when you stand up for yourself they might even give some respect towards you but in this case there is no respect, charisma or anything for you to gain, but you actually lose more and it will make you feel very weak and lower your confidence by a large margin. It becomes worse when you see the consequences you had to deal with like losing the teachers respect, getting in detention and being robbed of chances to maybe benefit your grades because the teacher sees you as a scumbag.

Now, if you don't know this, search it up just search demands and supplies and go on Google images and you will see two charts that contradict each other, and they determine the right amount of data for businesses. When they hit the middle that's when you make that choice but with the thing that

Beast Mode

I came to realize with human behavior is that we tend to choose to favor the social reputation side of things whenever we want to make a choice. Whenever you want to choose the social reputation side, ask yourself these questions, what do I want my social reputation to be? And then after that, you pick one side of the chart. It also includes your self-interest whether good or bad and for the other question for your choice making, will this be your logical side of choice making which is as I said what I need to do that I know I have to do? Or will this make me feel weaker by doing it and make me lose my competence and confidence? So in rejecting the joke and saying no, you basically create more honesty, integrity and character for yourself and if you choose your social reputation then you might be overall friendlier with some people after that but you'll lose more respect both between teachers and some students and the best part is that whatever you choose, whether your social reputation or logical thinking, you'll suffer from the consequences, which is so wonderful about life, even if you fail from a decision you'll learn from it.

Now, we'll get to our second option against peer pressure that I said was going to be being authentic and trust me it is as it sounds. It's called standing up for yourself and being authentic. So basically, living your own way of life and being assertive so nobody dares to even challenge your ideas. And this requires you to start early so that when peer pressure gets real, you will have already mastered this ideology. It's essentially being free and not letting others dictate how you live and not care about what they think about what you like to do because that's real freedom. For example, being peer pressured to buy expensive brands.

For example, let's just say that your family is not ideal financially and you are a girl, some other girls start buying expensive brands and you feel as if you are behind the competition, this is common with girls to be honest. It makes you feel extremely competitive against other girls and sometimes this can be a good type of competition if the end goal or motivation will add something to you so a human being but mostly it's just over insignificant stuff and the sense of competition can feel really toxic.

So as a young girl, you feel jealous and go ask your parents for money so then you can go and buy that expensive brand and you even know your family is not in an ideal position to buy those shoes, but you know since they're your parents they feel bad for you because you're their child so with all of the struggles, they give you the money and you just spend it. Now, perhaps this doesn't happen but actually, it's common amongst adolescents and I will point out some common flaws and mistakes for when people go under pressure in this type of peer pressure. First, it's absolutely immoral to do this when your family is in time of need and you know that, like I know that teenagers are dumb and can't understand but come on we know better, you're literally valuing an item over your family's comfort. Second, you shouldn't waste your money and for god's sake save some money, you won't know the value of it now, but when you become an adult you know why it matters. Peer pressure can force us to make absurd decisions comparing to our circumstances and we tend to complain about why we couldn't have it that way. Like you could say that why does she get to spend that much and her monthly allowance is that much while I can't have as much as

Beast Mode

her and you know. What we fail to understand is that life is full of hardships and that life is absolutely and I say absolutely not fair, so you're complaining about why she has more allowance than you, just suck it up, life will be full of inequality and people will stay rich, poor and have different circumstances, but just realize nobody has it perfect and that we all have a fair share of suffering however everything is changeable.

Like she might have more expensive clothing but that doesn't mean she's a better person or has no problems, she might have a lot of insecurities or not have friends, so just remember everybody has their strengths and weaknesses. Another thing you have to realize is that in life there will be things you can't change and when you can't change circumstances, you change your own decisions. So when you can't but want to buy those shoes, you overall reject peer pressure and not buy those clothes. That's the circumstance and the different decision that you made and that will also be one of those things that will increase your competence over time and shows that you have true courage.

Now, here's where the authenticity comes in, you've already talked about rejecting the pressure so what you do is that you become authentic and won't buy into the peer pressure and wear the same clothes you always do and this way it's just a huge backlash against the modern norms and not only that but it increases your competence, confidence, and charisma. You'll start regarding yourself as somebody who rejected the modern norms and who is strong-minded and competent who is not afraid to break the chains of trends and become superhuman.

Others will see more charisma in you and believe you're definitely somebody they can count on because of the charisma you have, they'll respect you because they think that you showed extreme courage to even try to reject modern norms and they'll see you as an elder and leader because of that and overall this charisma makes you more attachable. Now, not all people will think that, but most will.

This is why this way is authentic, you must be unique and original like human beings used to be and have the courage to reject modern trends and norms and basically, the reason you must do this fast is that after this nobody will even think about pressuring you.

Now, our previous way was if you wanted to be more authentic. Our third way requires vulnerability, which means it requires you to open up. For some people this might be hard including me because I'm more of an introvert with emotions which is ironic considering how much of an extrovert I am socially. Some people don't like to show vulnerability because we don't want others to have that power over us and I understand and agree with that, information and data is the new form of power, if you have information over someone's life, you basically have leverage over them. So that's why it's hard for people like me and others who are like me to open up because we feel like we will lose control and power in our lives if somebody takes the info from our lives and spills the information because then our reputation is ruined and everything becomes chaos.

So yeah that's how I see it but another perspective which is really important in my opinion is that you should talk about your emotions. It is scientifically proven that people who talk about their emotions feel better after it and as I have already stated mental health is really important. So, I recommend that everybody has at least one adult they really trust so if you have mental problems and social problems you can tell them because A: they have more experience than you and B because they can help you. I don't care which adult, could be your parents, one of your teachers, etc. just somebody you feel comfortable talking to and have a lot of trust in. Now, some of you may ask "can a friend work" and the answer to that is that it depends, since friends are really emotionally invested in you they might not want to hurt your feelings or even affect you in anyway so they just give you empathy which sucks because it helps you in the short run but doesn't fix the problem in the long run, so that's why adults are better it's because they give you logical advice.

And as I said mental health and problems are really important and peer pressure is not different, it can seriously boggle your mind and stress you and give you anxiety so yes it's important to sometimes talk with an adult you trust about how you feel because that will help you get your emotions out, if you're the type of person who likes to do that. I don't consult an adult all the times since I solve my problems on my own but if you think it's a good idea or is desperate than I would definitely say go for it because adults are way more experienced than us.

Now, as a little Timbit I think all of us are familiar with, one of the most common pressures in peer pressure include achievements and basically when you feel that someone else's lists of achievements outmatch yours or your parents think like that.

Now, if it's your parents with this ideology, then I can't help you other than give you the pointer of having a good close to heart conversation with them but if it's with you then that's solvable because most people know that this type of ideology is a type of toxic mentality that will bring you nothing more than misery because nothing will ever be enough for, you will always want something or an achievement somebody else has until you die, you will never get the joy of some moments in life.

However, as much as a secret to eternal happiness as it may look like to not care, I am against it because it turns off motivation and later on, I'll explain why I actually think that this type of thinking could be useful to your life. However as much as I like it, what I am against is over comparing yourself to others because it just brings worries and misery into your life.

Be disciplined, be authentic and don't over compare yourself to others, those are my top 3 rules for life, do them and you will have a happy life.

Back to comparing, another known attribute of comparing yourself to others is the common feeling of jealousy which will make you deluded and make you untruthful and it's like a virus, it slowly rips apart your life and morals, it makes you stop being grateful for what you already have an intern jealousy makes you want more resources of something even though you haven't used the resources you've already had.

Beast Mode

For example, social media. Now, I don't know if you know this or not, social media feeds off of jealousy because humans are so sneaky and we all think our lives are crap and want to look into others' lives and think how great it is and become jealous because humans like feeling victimized by nature, that's why feeling like you're offended or oppressed kind of feel good, because you can start pitying yourself. So yeah, I'd go as far to say that some people have social media just to check other's images and pity themselves even though the person who uploaded that photo themselves thinks that they also have a very bad life and it's just a cycle between all of the users.

Now, I'm going to use the resources example of how we don't use or maximize the resources we have but still want more of that resource. For example, we see a picture of our classmates on Instagram on how many friends they have and how happy they are with them, even though we have friends(resources) we don't spend as much time as we should with them, so intern without actually trying to further improve the relationships we have and being happy inside them, we want to get more average relationships and think those will help us other than a few meaningful relationships.

Sometimes sticking to what we have and improving it further, can give us more satisfaction and bring more joy into our lives than getting more things out of sensing greed and thinking that more resources will help us. Now, aside from resources and the jealousy of what others have and what we don't have, let's get more into achievements.

Comparison

"We're only envious of those already doing what we were made to do. Envy is a giant, flashing arrow pointing us toward our destiny."

– Glennon Doyle Melton

Sometimes in life, we will feel alone and lost because we compare our lives to somebody more successful and think "wow, I wonder what it would feel like to be that person" and we feel envious of them and we pity ourselves. This feeling is very natural and believes me it's almost a necessity to have this feeling at first if you wanna win the game of life and winning the game of life means being wise and being happy, having those two things in life is all you need. Now, how do you get happy?

Mostly when you reach the adult age, you get happy by completing and getting more accomplishments, so you don't die feeling useless. Now, the reason that accomplishments make you feel good is because in your mind accomplishing things is seen as a competitive game played with other people, parties competing for hierarchies, when you have more accomplishments than them and that makes you feel happy and special because you know that you're above other people, above everybody else in the social hierarchy.

Beast Mode

Now, the same thing goes for when this happens in reverse, when somebody has more accomplishments than you, except that feeling of glory, satisfaction and happiness of accomplishment is replaced with the feeling of pity, jealousy and the feeling of worthlessness because you feel that you're not worth enough and that you're at the bottom of the food chain. Now, as if other gurus would tell you to put this feeling of pity for yourself away and it will make you feel weak. Here's what I say, embrace it. As psychoanalysis says, when something feels bad or loses, it will come back with a greater vengeance. So, in this case, the feeling of pity in you comparing yourself to others will actually motivate you to be as good at that person, so it's more like motivation than that self-pity, that's why role models work so well.

However, I have an exceptional rule, stay in your own lane! For example, when I was on the rise of my writing career as you'd say and was getting very successful. One of my friends told me that his mom is telling him he should be more like me and however the matter may be that I am honored to have inspired somebody, but this is not the right way. Not everybody has to write a book to succeed, not everybody has to become rich or famous to become successful, success is what the person wants it to be. It comes down to what that accomplishment means for you, other than that it has no real-life value, the value is made by the individual. For example, you getting better at your marks so you can go to that dream university of yours could be equivalently successful in your opinion as my journey to Dragons' Den was, they could be on the same level of success. It's all in the individual!

So, we conclude that you shouldn't follow the exact steps of others or even be famous or rich to have success, it's the achievements that are special you hold the dearest to you that mean something and give your existence meaning. For example my accomplishments of getting this far in life at 14 mean a lot to me, and if that's your type of thing, you can try and do the same thing except in your own line of expertise, and if you don't want to follow my path that's fine, but just do things that fulfill the meaning of success for you. It has to also make you feel accomplished and so when you achieve them, they make you feel happy and the final goal for every human is to remove suffering from their lives and replace it with happiness and that's why I think the final level of happiness is having success on something that you value highly.

Take that feeling of self-pity and turn it into motivation and fill all the small holes in your life and achieve whatever that you so desire but can't have and once you achieve them, feel what a true beast feels like, accomplished, free and the final one that is the most important which is happy.

Here's a challenge I have for you, get a piece of paper and a pen and divide the paper in half with a line. In private write the name of a person that you're jealous of or more of a role model that makes you self-pity on the right and write your own name on the left and then list down in bullet points each accomplishment you or the role model has and then compare.

Now, for this to work, you need the role model to be someone that you're either jealous of or self-pity yourself from. Now, this could either be a celebrity, relative, friend, etc. After that sit-down and compare yourself and the ideal person accomplishment, don't you feel the self-pity? Don't you feel the jealousy? Don't you feel the anger? Don't you feel the worthlessness? Now, here's something interesting, I've taken you real deep haven't I, well welcome to reality, we all truly feel this inside but we cover it up with excuses and fake emotions and habits to cover what we truly feel. What we lack in the past, we seek in the future, when we lack the determination, we seek excuses, when we lack the logic for those excuses, we become liars and lying to yourself is the lowest you can be.

What your mind likes to quickly think is to feel oppressed because that's another form of defense that makes us feel good, you will feel as if you're the victim of a system that stopped you but now, instead of feeling oppressed and making excuses for the way you are, do this.

1st step: Accept responsibility, because it's the best weapon to be anti-delusional and it will intern make you a more mature adult as you grow. Accept that you were too busy wasting your time or you just didn't have enough courage to do something that could have made you feel more accomplished somewhere down the line, which could've intern made you feel morally and existentially happier or even made your life better if you had the courage to take it.

Whether a better connection with your friends or an opportunity you missed out on because you were too arrogant or weak to accept. You might feel a bit of uneasiness confessing to yourself, you know why? It's really hard for the mind to see itself as the victim in the situation and intern you have just broken that wall and have essentially gotten the rebirth mentally to see the world through the new perspectives.

Now, here's what I want you to do, on the back of that paper I want you to write down all the confessions you have done to yourself and then after I want you to sign the top right and write your name and last name and the date, this will be a covenant/contract between yourself to never lie to yourself and accept responsibility.

Here's another question you might ask yourself, what happens if I break the contract/covenant? Well, the answer is that the contract is between yourself and when you break a deal with yourself things rather get depressing and you will feel the lowest and weakest that you have felt in your life if you were serious about the contract for not lying to yourself because you know that you can't even keep a promise to yourself that you made with yourself.

Second step: Now, after confessing to never lie to yourself ever again, on another sheet, I want you to write these questions down then answer them clearly. First question, how much suffering is enough? How much more do you have to suffer from what you know you shouldn't be doing, which may be distractions for some, making excuses for others, how much more of what are you going to take until you change, how tired are you of feeling that weakness and helplessness, feeling like you're lower than everybody else in this world and being depressed, how much more of that desperate feeling are you going to take until you realize that you can't take it anymore. Now, second question, and since you're alone and it's just you, you have no fear, to be honest, unless you're a coward and even communicating with yourself feels uncomfortable because you know you're a hypocrite.

On a scale of 1 to 10 how satisfied are you with yourself and after that, I don't care how you rated yourself but just write down your weaknesses. Now, just look at the weaknesses and just think about how weak they make you feel and what measures you are willing to make to change them to make yourself feel less weak and more competent. Now, you either have the choice to ignore them and focus on your strengths and be dominant in those or focus on the weaknesses in your life so they will all equalize and cancel each other out.

Now, this could be a weak talent you have or a horrible relationship you have and those two make you feel weak or maybe you have a good relationship and you want to focus on that or that you want to get really good at playing the guitar even though you're already good at the guitar. The best part of this is there is no right answer, either one you choose matters except one thing which is the fact that you chose to do something in the first place and made up your mind. when we choose to do something, we put responsibility behind the action and responsibility is the feeling of assurance in ourselves that we give to the mind to choose to do something.

That responsibility is the antidote to the weaknesses in your life, it's the lack of assurance in yourself that causes blaming and if you can't choose and take responsibility for those actions how are you going to mature up, that's the problem with today's society the lack of responsibility. So, I don't care whether you chose to work on your strengths or to equalize your weaknesses, the importance is that you made a choice and that choice took some self-assurance and responsibility and that's what you're looking for.

I bet you're asking yourself, what happens if we chose the wrong thing and we screw up when we made that decision? Well, were teenagers, literally the time when we're turning into adulthood which is for more maturity development and more experiments, it doesn't matter if what you chose turned out to lead to something bad, sure I mean you will feel really bad at first but you know in your heart you trusted yourself and you had self-assurance so it's your fault and you have nobody else to blame but yourself, so instead of making excuses and blaming others you took responsibility and you will feel happy and strength inside, because you are mature and strong enough to know when you've failed and you accept the responsibility of the bad decision made by yourself and happily serve the consequences of what your action led up to in your life.

Now, the third step, on the back of that paper write down steps that will allow you to have more moral happiness in your life and will make you feel more competent, less weak and more confident. Write down how you will stop the moral and existential suffering and feel better about yourself and walk with your shoulders up high and stop blaming other people and stand up for yourself and take responsibility for yourself. Take that feeling of self-pity and turn it into motivation for the next action you will have to take.

After carefully planning out all the plans and doing these steps, keep them together either by stapling or flex tape and whenever you feel lonely, depressed or even about to give up on a dream of yours, take these papers out and look at them and look at how your once inferior-self wanted to make your life better and with just looking at those papers you will instantly feel better and you know you can't break the covenant/contact because that means you'll break your own trust with yourself and that's just pathetic.

Another method could even work better for some people than comparing yourself to others, which is also from Dr. Jordan Peterson, "Compare yourself with who you were yesterday and not others" Which in my opinion is absolutely brilliant but this also kind of goes with my last point. You comparing yourself to others will make you more motivated which in turn will make you a better person than yesterday because you'll be more accomplished in whatever area than yesterday. This will also be a more organized and humble approach to things because you don't really compare yourself to other people in this way of approach. So, you know that you're on plan. I would recommend that if you're a more organized type of person and don't want to make plans as you go, it really helps you stay on track.

Time and mind (not an inception reference)

"Attitude is a little thing that makes a big difference."

— *Winston Churchill*

Attitude will have a big impact on what you'll do. Different attitudes towards things or a more positive attitude lead you to success throughout your life. As this quote presents, Winston Churchill, one of the best politicians of our time could only end the evil reign of Nazi Germany in world war 2 by changing his attitude towards the war. He had a different approach to the Nazis than the previous prime minister Neville Chamberlain who thought they could have a peace treaty with them and tried to try a useless method known in politics as appeasement. Winston Churchill is a man I look up to in my life (even though he's dead) he's the resemblance of hope and courage against tyranny and chaos. The English were on the brink of getting conquered even after getting the miracle save of Dunkirk of 338,226 allied soldiers after Britain and France got annihilated by Germany and the whole country of France fell. Since the British were weak now, Hitler offered a peace treaty to Churchill. What comes next is an amazing response from Mr. Churchill himself. It shows that attitude can change a human and also inspire others and I know that some of you might say that these are politician words, but these are still inspiring.

Beast Mode

"We shall go on to the end, we shall fight in France, we shall fight on the seas and oceans, we shall fight with growing confidence and growing strength in the air, we shall defend our island, whatever the cost may be, we shall fight on the beaches, we shall fight on the landing grounds, we shall fight in the fields and in the streets, we shall fight in the hills; we shall never surrender."

That's the moment where it all started, and Germany went downhill just because of one man having the attitude of hope and also giving it to other (also the Soviet Union). Changing your attitude is a really useful thing because it has an impact on your mind and how you think.

The mind will have the biggest impact on your life because the different ways you think will affect the different actions you will take and those actions will have consequences, which is the beauty of life because whatever the consequence, good or bad, you learn something from your actions and those teachings could prevent you from future mistakes. So, if what you think or rather how you think will affect your actions, change your lifestyle and not your temporary actions.

You must develop the type of intelligence that is always self-aware of what its thinking and what it will do next, awareness is a very important thing in both life and communication. Like self-awareness is good to figure out the other person's limits, so what I usually do is I try to see what type of person the other person is in my first impressions with them. Strengths, weaknesses, whether they're aggressive or passive and how those will affect our current conversation and a possible future relationship, that's what awareness basically is.

The main reason you should pay attention and be aware of what you are thinking about it that as I said it earlier it affects your actions and you want your actions to be based on a set of morals and logic you have pre-determined and developed.

Believe me, developing a good moral system is really hard and it requires a lot of self-awareness, to judge every one of your actions. After you've done that and have developed a good self-awareness and can judge your actions, you're set to go for building good morals for yourself an intern making a better character for yourself. Now, there is another use for self-awareness, which as I said is filtering what you think so you can have a productive life. So how do you filter your thoughts? Well, you see which ones are not worth having and you try to forget them, this is a method I always use.

One of those types of thoughts I want to touch on and express is when somebody abuses, bullys or tortures you with their words and gets you down. So, here are two ways you can have a Mindshift in life if that's one thing you think about a lot and believe me mind shifts are extremely important in life. First, think to yourself that if what they're actually saying is legit and if it even deserves your attention. Like, don't use too much brain energy on comments that others make, that you literally know have any intention of helping you and just straight-up insult you.

Like sometimes people tell me, wow, you're a really garbage author and I was like ok thanks but what should I do to make my writing better and they just walk away. Like IF YOU'RE GONNA INSULT YOU BETTER GIVE ME SOME ADVICE ON WHAT I CAN DO BETTER NEXT TIME. So yes, I'm not gonna turn into a turtle and go in the corner of my room, go in a shell and think about those comments because I know the only intent the comment had in the first place was just to be an insult.

Use your head, you don't like the comment either question the person or ignore it, you don't like a relationship, break it, just don't waste precious brain energy on comments that other people make because people can either be impulsive, jealous or stupid. Like for me, I can't risk losing my precious focus and brain energy on other people either occupying my mind, wasting my time and making me do what I don't like and I encourage you to do the same. Pick a goal and dream your life, spend your brain energy on it and let nobody try to take that brain energy from you, in the end, you're going to be a mediocre adult and you will regret every time you gave a crap that you tried to please other people and let their useless comments get to you.

Do you know why success is so rare? It's because people don't have courage, you know why they don't? Because they spend their entire life, time and mental energy trying to please others, thinking about what others think of them and trying to fit in. Let's take me for example, there may be teens way smarter than me out there with the same circumstances I have, a good and supportive family, medium social class and etc. But out of them all, I was the one that decided to write a book, I was the only one that decided to sit in front of a monitor for an entire year so I can finish a goddamn book (two

Beast Mode

times), I mean I could've given up and been an ordinary teen but I didn't.

I took the courage to not be average, I had the courage to make those sacrifices and I got my results. We get so caught up with others life that we forget our own, don't care about what others think because it doesn't matter, you do your own thing and they might be laughing and doubting right now, but they won't be laughing when you become a legend in what you're doing and be somebody they will strive to be. They will never amount to anything in their lives because they're too mediocre and their courage and discipline limit how much they can achieve.

So the question is, are you going to "forgive" others for their insolence, not because you're Gandhi or Buddha but are you willing to forgive others because you can have enough mental energy to spend on your goals so later on you can use as a silent told you so and rub it in their face. Are you willing to remove things in your mind that spend useless brain energy and waste your time and put that energy and put that focus on goals that actually matter to you? Do you have enough courage to do that or are you going to be a coward and run from the true experience that life has to offer you?

Many people doubted me, told me I couldn't write well, I'm too stupid to even touch on a subject like success but you know what, I didn't sit in my room all day crying about what others said, I took the courage to even try harder to prove them wrong.

I took that brain energy I saved from not thinking about other's comments and put that energy into myself and tried to

Beast Mode

make something out of my life and myself and gradually built my competence up enough to also be an amazing public speaker. Now, I'm pretty sure those achievements shut those up who once laughed at me and doubted me.

Once you move your mental energy to positive things like your goals in life which are symbols of hope for a better future, you will automatically act more positive and getting better results because what you spend more time thinking about automatically paves the road in that direction.

If you think about other's comments and how they always think about you, you will have a negative mindset and that will instantly set you up for failure. Mind shifting is the first step to having a peaceful life and I demand you to have a Mindshift in your life because an individual and positive mindset is what you must succeed in your goals and dreams, not a negative one that's always thinking about others and how their thoughts, actions and comments attack your life. Take the courage to have that Mindshift in your life and not care about how others and everything affects you and have a Mindshift, I promise you, you will feel satisfied simultaneously.

It's the final countdown

The journey is never ending. There's always gonna be growth, improvement, adversity; you just gotta take it all in and do what's right, continue to grow, continue to live in the moment.

- Antonio Brown

So, my dear former once coward and current beast, are you ready to put everything that you've learned in this book to life. In life, 50% of things that you will eventually learn, are learned by mostly experience. So, go out there and try to achieve oncoming goals and dreams that you have and live life on your own terms after that.

The best part about life is that you learn by the consequences of your actions, so if something goes bad you will know because of the resulted outcome. And the human psyche is that we tend to not use information from other people they have experienced in that area. So, try to use my advice in this book and build a good foundation in yourself, after that whatever you do right or wrong will guide to your ultimate beast form, because we learn by experience.

I will not lie but the journey will be hard, you will have ups and downs and the downs are inevitable because you learn from them and you might think that you want to give up but, I'm gonna sound like William Wallace in Braveheart for a

Beast Mode

second. Dying in your beds many years from now, with the feeling of guilt and regret for all the opportunities you missed out in your life, would you be willing to trade all the days from this day to that, for one chance just one chance, to come back here and tell ourselves that the road to those dreams might be hard and that you might have lots of downs but that you are willing to sacrifice and have the courage to go on the route for your dreams.

You have to dream but take action for those goals, you can't just lay back on your chair and say "Shervin told me that I can live my life on my own conditions", no you can't do that, you need discipline. You need to have the courage to fight every day for your goals and make sacrifices so you can achieve those goals and dreams so one day you look in the mirror and say wow look at how weak I was and look at me now.

You also must be honest with yourself to build a better character and overall have more morals. Don't lie to yourself because that makes you feel weak and that instantly turns off your power to have good goal setting. When you're overall more honest with yourself you don't feel guilty of hypocrisy and not doing the right thing.

Also, don't be ignorant, be grateful and accept the little experiences in life. Wanna join a school club, do it, it's more knowledge and more knowledge will eventually give you more opportunities in life and those opportunities will be good memories and give you more wisdom.

Realize that you can't control everything because that's the most feeling of self-assurance you'll ever get, but realize that you can control some aspects of it like allowing people you want into your life and keeping those that you don't like out of your life, talking to people you want and ignoring the people you hate, being overall self-conscious but not too over-reliant on your feeling of control because when things go wrong and you realize that you never had actual control over any of it but it was only a perception of control, you will be scared and disappointed.

Also, don't think that school teaches you everything that you need to learn, spend your own time reading and learning more wisdom and everything about the world like relationships, social tips and how to be morally stronger as a person.

Be a beast and have the courage to do what you want to do, when you want to do it, how you want to do it. live life on your own terms, not by other terms, set your expectations high and get high results, put distractions away and spend more time with yourself. Others might waste their time on things that are distractions but not you because you have a vision and you will let nothing or anyone distract you from that.

Understand that courage is a vital necessity for success because people rarely have the courage to do what they want but if you have enough courage, responsibility, and discipline you can outplay anybody in the game of life and be a beast. They don't have courage because they're cowards and its overall easier not to succeed than to succeed that's why there are so many cowards.

Life is like a horse begging for a horseback ride, it's begging you to live your life with satisfaction and no regrets, it's begging you to have good morals and live with a good character and integrity. So, what are you waiting for, have the courage to accept the horseback ride and feel accomplished and be happier about your life in general! Remember not me, your parents, your friends or anybody else can change your future for you, it's only you who can take those steps, I only have one question, are you ready?

Manufactured by Amazon.ca
Bolton, ON